Advance praise for
The Financial Planner's Guide to Moving Your Practice Online: Creating Your Internet Presence and Growing Your Business

by Douglas H. Durrie

"**Financial advisors need to develop an Internet strategy now or risk losing their clients to advisors who already have.** *Moving Your Practice Online* shows you the best way to attract new clients and retain your existing customers by using the Web."

> JON MARKMAN
> Managing editor, MSN Money
> Author of the best-seller *Online Investing*

"Moving any business online can be an extremely challenging and daunting task, but Durrie validates the importance of establishing an online presence in this **practical and thorough** guide. **A financial planner's marketing must!**"

> JERRY DAVIS
> President and CEO
> LifeGoals Corporation

"**A terrific, timesaving reference** for any planner who wants to use the Web to get more business. This book is loaded with links to helpful sites and tips for using them."

> KIP GREGORY
> President
> The Gregory Group

"Doug Durrie presents **everything you need to know about doing business on the Internet in this concise, to-the-point work.** It is an excellent resource both for beginners and for those more experienced in the online world. If you want a quick crash course in what really matters and what really works online, buy this book!"

> TERRY L. BROCK
> Professional Speaker and
> Syndicated Columnist

THE FINANCIAL PLANNER'S GUIDE TO MOVING YOUR PRACTICE ONLINE

Other Planner Books from Bloomberg Press

Deena Katz on Practice Management:
for Financial Advisers, Planners, and Wealth Managers
by Deena B. Katz

Deena Katz's Tools and Templates for Your Practice:
for Financial Advisers, Planners, and Wealth Managers
by Deena B. Katz

Getting Started as a Financial Planner
by Jeffrey H. Rattiner

Best Practices for Financial Advisors
by Mary Rowland

Protecting Your Practice
by Katherine Vessenes, in cooperation with the
International Association for Financial Planning

Also of Interest

Clicking Through:
A Survival Guide for Bringing Your Company Online
by Jonathan Ezor

A complete list of our titles is available at
www.bloomberg.com/books

BLOOMBERG® WEALTH MANAGER magazine is the premiere
professional information resource for independent financial planners and
investment advisers who are serving clients of high net worth.
See wealth.bloomberg.com or call 1-800-681-7727.

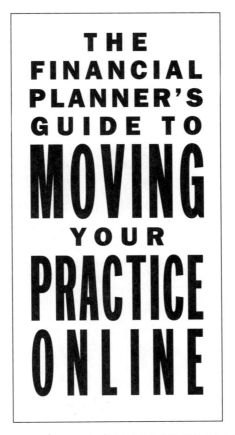

THE FINANCIAL PLANNER'S GUIDE TO MOVING YOUR PRACTICE ONLINE

CREATING YOUR INTERNET PRESENCE AND GROWING YOUR BUSINESS

DOUGLAS H. DURRIE

BLOOMBERG PRESS

PRINCETON

Books are available for bulk purchases at special discounts. Special editions or book excerpts can also be created to specifications. For information, please write: Special Markets Department, Bloomberg Press.

This publication contains the author's opinions and is designed to provide accurate and authoritative information. It is sold with the understanding that the author, publisher, and Bloomberg L.P. are not engaged in rendering legal, accounting, investment-planning, or other professional advice. The reader should seek the services of a qualified professional for such advice; the author, publisher, and Bloomberg L.P. cannot be held responsible for any loss incurred as a result of specific investments or planning decisions made by the reader.

First edition published 2001
1 3 5 7 9 10 8 6 4 2

Library of Congress Cataloging-in-Publication Data

Durrie, Douglas H., 1949-
    The financial planner's guide to moving your practice online: creating your Internet presence and growing your business / Douglas H. Durrie & Securities America, Inc.
        p. cm. — (Bloomberg professional library)
    Includes index.
    ISBN 1-57660-091-2 (alk. paper)
    1. Financial planners–United States–Marketing. 2. Electronic commerce–United States. 3. Internet marketing–United States. I. Securities America. II. Title. III. Series.

HG179.5 .D877 2001
332.1'0285'4678–dc21   2001029518

Edited by Rhona Ferling

Book design by Don Morris Design

CONTENTS

Acknowledgments

THIS BOOK WOULD NOT BE POSSIBLE without the efforts of a number of the professional staff at Securities America Financial Corporation. I would like to thank Janine Wertheim, Kirk Hulett, and Dennis King for the content and organizational suggestions that make this a user-friendlier book for the financial service professional. I also want to thank Doreen Griffith, Roxanne Wieland, Diana Criser, and Aaron Spahr for reviewing the book for technical accuracy and understandability. Ann Welsh deserves special recognition for her review of the book's accuracy regarding compliance and regulatory guidelines as well as for much of the content in the chapter on regulation of the Internet. Special thanks go to Derek Peterson for his general editing, content contributions and layout suggestions. Finally, I want to thank Roger Smedley and Aubrey Jenson of Smedley Financial Services for giving me invaluable input from an independent representative's perspective.

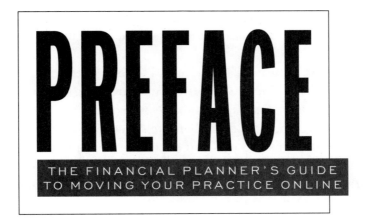

PREFACE

THE FINANCIAL PLANNER'S GUIDE TO MOVING YOUR PRACTICE ONLINE

INTERNET, ONLINE, WEB-BASED, virtual, Web site, cyber,

e-mail, chat room … The words bombard us from every

direction. Dot-com companies flash across our con-

sciousness like shooting stars. One minute you're asking,

"What was the name of that company?" and two minutes

later they've gone public for several billion, then four

minutes after that they go bust, all without ever showing

a profit. The financial world has been turned on its head. Investors are going online in droves, placing trades through discount brokers that didn't exist three years ago, and getting burned. Yet, even the staid and conservative wire houses are reinventing themselves as cyberbrokers.

Is there a future for the financial adviser in this new world of instant information and do-it-yourself investing? The answer is a most emphatic "Yes!" This book is your road map; it lays out the steps in building a successful online practice. However, in order to succeed in this new age, you need to understand the new rules of the road.

◆ **Your client probably has or shortly will have a computer.** The Commerce Department found in its latest survey of computer usage that the share of households with computers rose from 42.1 percent in December 1998 to 51 percent in August 2000—a total of 53.7 million households.

◆ **Your client is probably online or will be shortly.** The number of households with Internet access also soared, hitting 41.5 percent in August 2000, up from just 26.2 percent in the 1999 survey.

◆ **Your client probably has or will have an online brokerage account.** There were nearly 3 million online full-service brokerage accounts in 1999. This number is expected to more than quadruple by 2004 (making up approximately half of all full-service accounts). But your competition will do just as well, with online discount brokerage accounts and online bank accounts roughly tripling.[1]

The advent of online brokerages has made for a much more savvy and demanding investor than in years past. Your clients want to understand their investments, and they want to be more actively involved in the investment process.[2] They are also more willing to take risks.[3] In addition, your most affluent clients are likely to be among the earliest users of online brokerage accounts.[4] More importantly, investors now have the tools to take a more active role. There are many examples of high-quality, investor-oriented sites. If you haven't taken the time to check out what your clients may be looking at before they talk to you, maybe you should:

MSN MoneyCentral Investor SuperModels site: http://money

central.msn.com/articles/invest/models/5249.asp. This is just a small portion of Microsoft's free site that contains one of the most sophisticated, easy-to-use online stock and fund screening and modeling programs found anywhere. Besides including the models developed by Jon Markman, the software can be configured to include just about any screening parameter that the user wishes.

ClearStation technical and fundamental analysis site: http://www.clearstation.com. ClearStation is another highly sophisticated and free investor site. This site combines portfolio management with investment education and the essentials of technical analysis, fundamental analysis, and community discussion.

Multex Investor Network independent investment research site: http://multex.multexinvestor.com. Multex provides, at no cost, the same research reports it offers on its institutional site, with only a fourteen-day delay. Merrill Lynch's and Goldman Sachs's sites also now offer their research to clients only. However, becoming a client requires only that the investor open an account, not purchase anything.

IPO.com initial public offerings site: http://www.ipo.com. IPO.com is the leading provider of free information about initial public offerings. In addition, it offers free access to the entire Securities and Exchange Commission's EDGAR (electronic data gathering analysis and retrieval) site's business, financial, and competitive information about public companies. This IPO information equals any available outside the wire houses.

Monitored investor community sites where company, stock, and investment information can be shared: Some of the best are *Silicon Investor* (http://www.techstocks.com), *ClearStation, Motley Fool* (http://www.fool.com), and *MoneyCentral* (http://money central.com). You may be surprised at the sophisticated level of the investor discussions found here.

Mutual fund screeners, fund reports, and portfolio trackers: Some of the best are *SmartMoney.com* (http://www.smart money.com), *MoneyCentral,* and *Morningstar.com* (http://www. morningstar.com). These sites offer both free and fee-based services that very nearly match those available to the professional.

However, even with all these changes, the picture of the twenty-first-century investor is not uniform. In fact, investors fall into three basic types. First is the new and most rapidly growing group, the do-it-yourself online investor. The Internet has made do-it-yourself investing much easier, and now all your neighbors think they can make money in the stock market. Guess what? Some of them can! In this new marketplace, your challenge is to be able to tell which investors really do belong on their own and which don't. Even when investors are skilled enough to handle their own investments, there are still services you can offer to support them, including long-term financial planning, business planning, portfolio analysis, and asset management advice. However, you need to recognize that the services you offer won't be focused on helping them place trades—that business is gone.

The second group is composed of investors who simply don't have time to do their own investing. They may or may not have the skills to invest on their own; they simply don't have the interest. Does this mean that this group will be happy with a traditional approach to brokerage? Probably not. While they may not want to do the actual investing, they will still want the instant information and interactive service that the Internet offers. This change is more in how you do business with them than in the type of business you do.

The final group are the uninformed investors who shouldn't do their own investing (even if they want to). This group presents your greatest challenge. Here you must tread lightly while you teach, guide, and monitor their efforts. These investors now have all the tools they need to invest on their own, but they don't understand how to invest wisely. Without you, they jump into day trading with both feet (and lose money big time) or spend their rent money investing online because they heard about some dot-com company on TV. Alternatively, they may run from the Internet revolution and become convinced that banks are the only safe place for their money (and miss all those other opportunities).

So how, in this brave new world, do you reach these new groups of clients, service existing clients, and continue to build your clients' portfolios? The answer is to use the same powerful tools that are changing the makeup of your prospects and clients to

The Three Types of Investors

Type of Investor	Type of Advice Wanted
Skilled Do-It-Yourself Investor	Long-term financial planning, business planning, portfolio analysis, asset management advice, etc.
"I Haven't the Time" Investor	The same long-term advice but with a focus on making it easier and more efficient for them to do business with you.
Clueless Investor	Education, ongoing guidance, and monitoring.

change the way you do business. Does this mean you should immediately drop all other forms of marketing and move everything online? No. Although the consumer landscape is changing rapidly, we will never be at the point where the Internet is the medium of choice for reaching all clients. However, the time is rapidly approaching when the majority of your clients are going to expect online service from you! Now is the time for you to begin to explore these new online tools.

What are these new tools? Read on ...

THE
FINANCIAL
PLANNER'S
GUIDE TO
MOVING
YOUR
PRACTICE
ONLINE

INTRODUCTION

THE FINANCIAL PLANNER'S GUIDE TO MOVING YOUR PRACTICE ONLINE

Where Do You Start?

THE NET ALLOWS YOU to develop some very creative strategies. However, like anything new, it can be both intimidating and a bit overwhelming. Thus, I have broken this book into two parts. The first section, "Basic Strategies," lays out some successful methods and recommended resources that you can simply incorporate into your marketing. The second portion of the book,

"Advanced Cybermarketing," is designed as a reference to allow you to develop your own unique strategies, and it includes a wealth of resources that may be useful to your online approach.

If the Internet and online marketing are new to you, I suggest you start by following the steps laid out in this section. As you become more adept at cybermarketing, expand your horizons and add some of the concepts and techniques discussed in "Advanced Cybermarketing."

OK, so what is the first step?

Developing an Internet Marketing Plan

TO PARAPHRASE a well-worn movie line: "Plan! I don't need no stinking plan!" Too often this seems to be the approach to online marketing. This kind of thinking results in marketing that wastes your time and money and simply doesn't work. Like any other part of marketing, Internet marketing begins with a written marketing plan. The first step is to figure out what you intend to use the Internet for. Start by asking yourself the following questions. Be sure to jot down your answers. For more help on how to answer these questions, see Chapter 5, "Reach Out and Touch Someone."

◆ **Have you determined your target audience?** This is your first step. Constantly working your existing clients and your primary source of leads for referrals will shape your online marketing as well. Working a particular market niche (401(k), college students, the affluent, small businesses, etc.) will also affect how you use online services. If you target a particular demographic (age, sex, ethnic background, married, etc.) you need to reach the portion of the Web that appeals to these groups. Keep your target audience in mind as you answer the remaining questions.

◆ **Are you going to use the Internet for servicing existing clients?** Which client service activities do you want to support? This question addresses whether and to what degree you allow existing clients to handle many servicing activities online. Examples include downloading forms and viewing client accounts.

◆ **Do you plan to directly prospect for new clients online?** This is the online equivalent of direct mail or the cold call. The most obvious example is simply purchasing an e-mail list and sending an e-mail. However, be sure you study the section on "Active prospecting"—there are some major limitations on Internet cold calls.

◆ **Is the Internet an advertising tool for you?** Your goal with this approach is simply to get a client or prospect to respond. Examples might include banner ads placed on other sites, regular e-mail contacts with your client list, or a Web site where you have online client tools that notify you when they are used.

◆ **Do you plan to sell using the Internet?** Don't confuse this question with the prior one. This means you are actually planning on using the Internet to close a sale. An example might be a Web site where you and your clients go online together and you walk them through a sales presentation. Another example might be an online sales seminar where people can pay you online.

◆ **Do you plan to have a Web site?** Is your site to be used as part of the prospecting, selling, or service process? A Web site can help you reach one or more of these goals. Remember your site can have more than one purpose.

◆ **Do you plan to use e-mail?** Is e-mail to be used as part of the prospecting, selling, or service process? Like Web sites, e-mail can accomplish one or more of these objectives. Your e-mails can have multiple purposes.

◆ **Do you plan to advertise your Web site or place links on other Web sites?** Banner ad space is available on a variety of sites that reflect different prospect interests. Some of these may be good choices for advertising. If you have a Web site, you might choose to have your site linked to others with high traffic from the type of prospect you are looking for.

◆ **Do you plan to list your site and/or office with online directories or search engines?** There are several means of listing your business online. Being on a list may or may not involve a link to a Web site. There are also specialized directories by industry, occupation, or interest. Search engines and online directories are the main method by which people locate Web sites online, and thus they draw heavy traffic.

With your answers to these questions, you should be equipped to begin writing your plan. Keep it simple. Start by coming up with an overall strategy that will drive your plan. Following this section are some examples of Internet marketing strategies. They will help you flesh out your thinking so you can summarize the strategy in your plan. This Internet marketing plan should be short (no more than two pages). Do not create your Internet plan in a vacuum. Whatever you decide to do, it must complement your existing marketing efforts. For example, if you plan direct mail or ads, ensure that your Internet marketing is timed to match and that there are cross-references in both mediums.

Appendix A contains both an outline of how to develop an online marketing plan and a sample marketing plan (using the customer service strategy described in the next section) to act as a model for constructing your own plan. In addition, there are several sites that can help you in developing a marketing plan (or business plan if you still don't have one—shame! shame!). Two of the better sites are Bplans.com (http://bplans.com) and Center for Business Planning (http://businessplans.org). If you would like additional help in developing marketing ideas, a good site is Marty Baird's advisormarketing.com (http://advisormarketing.com). This Web site is specifically for financial advisers and allows you to direct specific marketing questions to Marty.

As you make your plans, consider whether you have enough staff skilled in the use of the Internet to assist you. If the answer is no, you don't have to do it yourself or wait until your current staff is trained. Another option is to hire a "virtual assistant." This is a new concept: You outsource your staffing needs through an online source such as AssistU (http://www.assistu.com). You can hire executive-level administrative support that work for you handling tasks like database management, Web site development, mass e-mail, and other more traditional administrative tasks via the Internet. Also, talk to your broker-dealer to see what Internet or electronic support programs he may offer.

After reading this book, keep in touch with new ideas and developments by checking www.movingyourpracticeonline.com.

BASIC
STRATEGIES

☞ **HELPFUL HINTS:** Look for the helpful hints scattered throughout Part 1. These give you some general insight or assistance in dealing with marketing online. These hints apply not only to the strategy in which they appear but to any strategy.

HERE ARE SOME BASIC strategies that you can use in developing your Internet marketing plan. Now, don't get too rigid in your thinking here; these strategies are not mutually exclusive. They are also purposely written with as little overlap as possible to make their differences more apparent. However, you can adopt more than one or merge several together. In fact, be sure you read the first three strategies. Many of the techniques used in them are also used in the narrower niche marketing strategies that follow. Remember, you also need to fully integrate these online approaches with the more traditional sales and marketing approaches you have been using all along.

CHAPTER

CUSTOMER SERVICE

LET'S SAY YOUR MAIN GOAL is to create a strong personal relationship with your clients, and you feel you should get the bulk of your new clients from referrals. You also find that most of your new business comes from additional sales to your existing clients. Well, not surprisingly, this means you have a heavily *client-focused* marketing strategy.

To move this strategy online, you need to start using online technology as a tool to mine your existing customer database for new business, increase personalization in your communications, and enable more efficient customer support. Everything you do, including what you do online, should focus on strengthening the relationship between you and the client. The principal online channels used in this strategy are a business Web

> ☞ **HELPFUL HINT:** A Web site is not, in and of itself, a strategy; it is a channel of communication. So simply putting up a site doesn't accomplish anything (no matter how great it looks and how well it functions). Unless you integrate it into an overall marketing and communications strategy, it is unlikely to have much impact on either sales or service.

site, an administrative mini–Web site, e-mail, Webcasting services, and a contact management system. Below are the steps necessary to develop this strategy.

Develop a Strategic Web Site

FOR A CUSTOMER SERVICE STRATEGY, your site needn't be unique, but it must be extremely user-friendly, and its usability must be tailored to your industry. Thus, you need a site designed by skilled developers familiar with the financial services industry. A site designed by a specialist in developing financial service template sites is probably best. Template sites have many of the standard service features you'll need on your site already prepackaged. Among those specializing in such sites, Financial Profiles' Profiles Online offers one of the lower cost and most robust options (http://financial profiles.com/products/advisor-Websites/default.asp). This type of site allows you to select from a broad array of functions, content, and layout options. They also have the advantage of an online compliance review that greatly speeds the site approval and updating process. (See "Web Site Developers," Chapter 7, for more information and other options for site development.)

You have a number of things to consider when creating your own variations on such a template site. Since your purpose is to reinforce the client relationship, the content you choose should reflect your professionalism, expertise, and concern for the customer. Your site should contain the following elements. (Note: these and other related topics are covered in much greater detail in "Content of a Typical Rep Site," page 118 in Chapter 6.)

☞ **HELPFUL HINT:** I strongly urge you to avoid the temptation to build the site yourself. Although concerns about cost and time may initially make this idea attractive, the reality is that site maintenance and subsequent compliance review are very time-consuming. You are an expert in financial services; you need to focus on your strengths. Therefore, you should spend your valuable time on your business strategies, not on becoming a Web developer.

◆ **Rep information.** You need a short bio highlighting your experience and any specialized expertise you possess. Don't get too carried away; this isn't a résumé, so a couple of paragraphs should suffice. However, the tone is important. Don't be too formal. You want to come across as warm and inviting.

You also need to have a list of your licenses, where you are approved to do business, and any professional designations you have acquired. Make sure the information is prominently displayed so you don't create compliance problems for yourself later. Remember, the whole world has access to your site.

For a customer service orientation, be sure you reinforce your commitment to service in writing; a service pledge or promise is a good idea. For example: "I promise to return all phone calls and reply to all e-mails within twenty-four hours," "I review all my clients' portfolios quarterly." That said, however, you *must* be prepared to go to extraordinary lengths to stand by any pledge you make. Once it's in writing, your customers will hold you accountable.

◆ **Company or firm information.** Include a description of your firm. This is particularly important if your practice has a specialty or focus. But again, concentrate on emphasizing the way you build long-term relationships with your clients. If it is appropriate to your community identity, include a description of your broker-dealer. You may even want to include an online map to your office(s).

◆ **Financial planning tools, market data information, and other interactive functions.** As much as possible, you want your clients to interact with your site once they arrive. The best way to make that happen is to give them something interesting to do. This can range from providing calculators to help them determine how much they need to save for college to quotes on their favorite stocks to a complete needs analysis form. Pick tools that assist you in providing better service rather than those that promote particular products or investment strategies.

Remember that the purpose of these interactive functions is to strengthen the client's relationship with you. So be sure your selections are consistent with this message and provide value to the client. The number and type of options are limited to the site developer's list, and you can choose which ones you want as part of the site template's setup.

◆ **Life, annuity, and/or mutual fund information.** If you have a particular product or group of products that are popular with your clients, include a link to additional information. However, avoid placing too much emphasis on product. In this strategy, product is the solution—you don't lead with it. Again, your company's approved product list and what is available from the site developer determine your selection of links.

◆ **Client account access and/or client trading.** Client account access is a critical piece for this strategy, since it is the primary site function that will attract the client. More than anything else, clients want information about their investments. This not only gives the client a reason to come to your site, it also is a reason to return on a regular basis.

◆ **An additional attraction might be client trading.** This option will depend on your and your broker-dealer's philosophy regarding direct client trading. Some broker-dealers have special client agreements that allow the rep to continue to manage a client's account but allow some level of client trading. Remember that many of your clients may already have an online account through a discount broker. Many of these firms are beginning to offer either online financial planning or an online adviser. Offering a competitive online trading service through your site may be a good way to prevent a potential client loss.

◆ **Ability to refer a friend.** As with any client contact, don't forget to ask for referrals. Although you could simply ask visitors for names and addresses, it is less intimidating and you get better information if you have a form that guides the visitor through the referral process.

◆ **E-mail contact information.** Your site should make it easy for the client to contact you via e-mail. But be sure to include your other contact information as well (phone, fax, address, etc.)

◆ **Events calendar.** If you are going to be holding seminars or workshops, be sure site visitors know when and where they are to be held. If you have additional information or a separate site devoted to the seminar or workshop, include a link to the site. For a service-oriented strategy, this is also a good place to list community events to show you're involved in the community. This is especially important if you are an active participant. Invite clients to attend and look you up. Don't just list the event; include a description of it, plus the reason this is such a great cause or event, and encourage visitors to participate. If the organization has a Web site, include a link to it.

◆ **Newsletters and articles.** If you plan to write your own newsletter and/or articles or plan to have third-party content available, you need sections for these. The content should keep reinforcing your commitment to providing quality and timely service. Again, avoid articles that tout product or investment strategies. A better focus is needs analysis, asset management, or financial planning. This section of the site can also be used to supplement a printed newsletter, allowing clients to select whether they receive your newsletter in printed form or by e-mail. Again, newsletter options on a template site are easily updatable and allow regular content changes.

Consider a Mini Site for Online Forms

MANY BROKER-DEALERS OFFER their administrative forms in a portable document format, or PDF, version (some in a variation that can be completed online). If your broker-dealer offers this option, you will want to create a link to a small administrative site

THE FINANCIAL PLANNER'S GUIDE TO MOVING YOUR PRACTICE ONLINE

> ☞ **HELPFUL HINT:** No matter how professional a site developer is and no matter how many good sites he or she has developed, you are still providing most of the content yourself. Take the time to make sure your content is well written and interesting to the reader. Then, change your site's content frequently—at least monthly. Nothing is more boring and nothing will drive clients away faster than static content. For more tips on site design, see Chapter 6, "What Makes a Good Site Good?"

that you can maintain. Most Internet service providers (ISPs) offer some amount of free Web space (for more information on Web site hosting, see the section on hosting online sales seminars beginning on page 78, Chapter 5). As long as this space can be password protected, you can post forms on this site and then notify your clients via e-mail, with instructions on how to complete the form and a link back to your mini site. You or your staff can even use this method in combination with a simultaneous phone call, allowing you to walk your clients through completing the form.

This has several advantages over mailing the forms. First, you no longer need a supply of forms since the PDF version is available for multiple clients. Second, you will know when the client completed and/or printed the form since the ISP maintains a record. Third, if the form can be completed online, there is no mail delay in getting the information from the client (though if a signature is required, you will need to wait for the printed, signed version to arrive before processing). Fourth, if you walk the client through the completion of the form, you will have a smaller chance of errors. For more information, see the "Online Forms" section in Chapter 9 on page 180.

◆ **Buy or lease a contact management system with automated e-mail capability.** The best solution is to use a system that is integrated with your broker-dealer's back-office system. This allows you to access a much more robust database of information about your clients. An example of such a system is Securities America's SABroker Client Manager.

Most contact management systems now have a location for an e-mail address. However, not all of them can automate an e-mail campaign in the same way they can a printed mailing campaign. Most online strategies require this capability to be truly efficient. If you have an existing Internet or software-based contact management system, be sure it has the capability to store e-mail addresses, store e-mail messages for future delivery to multiple clients, and integrate the contact information and data contained in the contact manager into those e-mails. For more contact management options, see the section "Staying in Touch With Your Clients," beginning on page 102 in Chapter 5.

◆ **Collect e-mail addresses for your current client base.** The latest Commerce Department survey estimates that nearly 42 percent of your clients are already online and that nearly 80 percent of them use e-mail. When you consider that this number increased by 40 percent last year alone, you will recognize that this is a distribution channel you cannot ignore.

You may already have some e-mail addresses in your current client files. However, e-mail addresses change frequently, so you need to make sure your list is up-to-date. You can do this over time as part of your regular service calls or send out a postcard mailing periodically asking for e-mail addresses and address changes. You can then use an e-mail address search to fill in any missing e-mail addresses. An excellent search is WhoWhere? People Finder (http://www.whowhere.lycos.com); it even includes the client's home address, phone number, and e-mail provider. For more on e-mail addresses, searches, and e-mail marketing, see "Direct E-Mail Marketing," Chapter 3.

◆ **Configure your contact management system to automatically send out regular e-mails to all your clients.** Always provide an e-mail reply link on your e-mail that allows the client to opt out of your regular e-mails. If you don't provide this, you can be accused of spamming (see "Legal and Ethical List Management and Spamming Issues" on page 76, in Chapter 5). For clients who don't have an e-mail address or prefer to be contacted by mail, have your contact manager notify you to send the communications listed below via regular mail.

◆ **Send short personal e-mails for birthdays, holidays, anniversaries, graduations, or other events.** Messages can be made up in advance and stored in your management system. The management system will add the names and any specific client information needed to personalize the e-mail from its database. You are probably doing something like this already with regular mail. However, regular mail involves staff time plus costs for postage and mailing. Both time and cost are reduced by using e-mail instead. You can also be much more creative with an e-mail (color, animation, and even sound). The cards can also be interactive. This makes your message more memorable.

Even if you can't integrate scheduled e-mail messages into your contact management system, there are a number of online card companies that can develop personalized messages for you. Most of these vendors offer automated scheduling services, although mass mailings are not yet possible. (However, some of the latest contact management services plan to integrate vendors' cards into their automated systems). Examples of such online card companies include Hallmark (http://www.hallmark.com) and Blue Mountain (http://www.bluemountain.com). If nothing else, they can give you some great ideas for your own e-mails.

◆ **Send regular e-mails to the top 20 percent of your clients soliciting referrals.** Since the best sources of new business are your existing clients, you need to be proactive in soliciting new clients from your best customers. E-mail is a particularly good medium for referrals since you can include a link back to your mini site with an online form the client can complete—far fewer steps for them and instant information for you. Your contact management system can automate and streamline the referral request process while still personalizing the message.

◆ **Send a regular e-mail newsletter link (monthly or quarterly) to your clients.** The newsletter resides on your Web site, so the e-mail is merely a short enticing summary of the high points covered in the online newsletter with links back to those portions of the newsletter on your site. This is much easier for the clients to digest than the online version and allows them to pick the content they are interested in hearing more about. Such an approach also lowers your costs because you need print and mail newsletters only for clients who insist on receiving them in print form.

◆ **Schedule a regular e-mail reminder (semiannual) to do a portfolio review with your clients.** The e-mail will include both the reminder and a link back to an online financial planning data entry form that the client can complete before your meeting and an appointment scheduler for the client to complete. This eliminates a lot of telephone tag by you and your staff.

◆ **Schedule an online portfolio review with remote or low-networth clients.** Obviously, the most effective way to review a portfolio analysis is to do it face-to-face. However, for clients who have a low net worth, are located far away, have family groups in different parts of the country, or have unusual or busy schedules, there are now online services that offer virtual-meeting facilitation. One of the better services for small meetings is Epiphany's iMeet (http://imeet.com). The company offers free use for fewer than five users and less than sixty minutes. This can be a great time- and cost-saver if your clients live some distance away

☞ **HELPFUL HINT:** Always provide a link back to your Web site. All client or prospect e-mails should have one thing in common: they invite the customer to visit your Web site through a link embedded in the e-mail. This includes all e-mail marketing programs and all regular e-mail correspondence. This is critical if you want to build traffic to your site. Even if you've sent out regular mailings because you had no e-mail address or a client or prospect has opted out of your e-mail program, include the Web site link address. It is very possible for someone to have an e-mail address that an e-mail search can't find (e.g., the e-mail may be under the name of only one family member) or for an individual to have computer access but no e-mail address (through work, for instance).

or time constraints make scheduling an appointment difficult. This service allows you and your client to simultaneously view any Windows-based software (such as financial planning software) and communicate using online chat or a simultaneous phone call. It is also possible to create a virtual white board, where you can share a concept online and both you and your client can contribute ideas directly to screens that both can see.

CHAPTER

CLIENT ACQUISITION SEMINARS

2

YOU MAY HAVE DEVELOPED or purchased a highly successful seminar system and have a regular cycle of seminars that you conduct throughout the year. These seminars can constitute the principal method you use to reach new customers and to develop additional business from your existing clients. Your main goal is to enhance your reputation as an expert in the topics covered by your seminars and thereby create and strengthen relationships with both prospects and clients. In this case, you have a heavily *expertise-* or *education-focused* marketing strategy.

This Internet strategy uses online technology to enhance an existing seminar prospecting strategy. Your focus here is to enhance your perceived expertise, maximize seminar participation, increase the frequency of seminars, lower costs, and improve the follow-up over traditional seminars. All of this should result in an increase in the number of seminar follow-up appointments and sales. The principal online channels used in this strategy are a specialized seminar Web site, Webcasting conference services, e-mail, and a contact management system. Below are the steps necessary to develop this strategy.

Developing Web Sites

FOR A SEMINAR STRATEGY, you need a highly focused site, with different sections for each unique seminar. The site's only purpose is to support and promote seminars. Do not attempt to service clients or provide nonseminar-related functions on this site. In addition, these types of sites have functions on them that are unique to seminars (both live and Webcast).

Either a generalist developer or one with specialized knowledge of our industry can develop these types of sites. However, those with previous seminar site design and/or financial service industry experience are more likely to understand your needs. Among those with industry experience, AdvisorSites offers securities-oriented custom sites that can be designed to your specifications (http://www.advisorsites.com/advisorsites/index.html).

AdvisorSites offers the unique advantage among custom site builders of an online compliance review. Seminar sites are generally quite small, with sections added and deleted with each change of seminar theme. This also means you must be able to create sites quickly and then change content rapidly and easily. Having a struc-

> ☞ **HELPFUL HINT:** Avoid trying to do too much with your Web site. Web sites that attempt to "cover all the bases" end up being vague and unfocused. The client or prospect should come away from your site with a clear understanding of who you are and what you offer them. This does not mean they will know your children's first names or be forced to read through a list of the 2,000 mutual funds. The K.I.S.S. principle applies—Keep it simple, stupid!

tured online method to make content changes and an automated compliance review approach greatly speeds the site creation, updating, and approval processes. (See "Web Site Developers," Chapter 7, for more information and additional options for both generalist developers and specialist developers.) As mentioned before, do not attempt to build a complex site like this by yourself.

A seminar site's purpose is to build interest in the event and to make it easy to register. To accomplish this, you need a number of basic components (additional information on specialized sites is available in "Building Specialized Niche Sites," Chapter 6, page 135):

◆ **Main page.** Your introductory page should include the seminar title, an online "hook" that attracts prospects to the seminar, five or six important learning points, any incentives or premiums received for attendance, seminar dates, and the location. Also, list the speakers and/or any third-party sponsors. Most of the items on this page should be linked to the more detailed information located on later pages (see below). You will also want links to the seminar synopsis, speaker bios, agenda, registration information, Webcast site, and your other sites.

◆ **Seminar synopsis.** Give a brief summary of what the seminar will cover. Expand on the learning points and tell prospects how the seminar specifically benefits them and who ought to attend.

◆ **Speaker biography.** All speakers need a short bio highlighting their experience in the topic area and any related expertise they possess. Speakers involved in sales of products or services also need to have a list of licenses, including where they are approved to do business.

◆ **Agenda.** Provide a complete agenda, including topics, presenter (if different), and times, in printable form (usually PDF format).

◆ **Registration information.** Include a phone, fax, and e-mail link for more information. You can also include a Web site link to an online registration form that should include spaces for the attendee's name, others attending, company (if appropriate), address, city, state, zip, work phone, home phone, fax number, and e-mail address. If you plan to serve lunch, include a place for listing dietary requirements. If you plan to charge for the seminar, include all cost information on the form.

Another option is to use a Webcast application service provider (described below) for registration. Such a service can handle the reservation process entirely online for the virtual seminar (and in some cases, the in-person seminar as well). Some ASPs can also handle seminar payment and collection online.

◆ **Location.** If your seminar is to be simulcast in person and online, you will want to include an online map to the seminar location. If the site is well known or has desirable features, include photos of the facility and/or meeting rooms.

◆ **Sponsor information.** If your seminar has a sponsor (e.g., mutual fund company, carrier, etc.) include a link to the sponsor's site for further information. Note that many companies now have special sections of their Web sites that are specifically designed to complement the sales efforts of representatives. However, others do not and thus may include things like pitches to purchase their products directly or links to discount brokers. So be careful. Be sure you know what is being said on the sponsor's site before you agree to provide a link.

◆ **Incentives.** If you offer some special incentive or premium to encourage attendance or early registration, include a link to information explaining what is being offered, along with graphics or photos as appropriate.

◆ **Encourage referrals.** Just as with a client service site, don't forget to ask for referrals. In this case the referrals are others who might be interested in attending the seminar.

◆ **Events calendar.** If you are going to be holding future seminars or workshops, be sure the potential attendees know when and where. If you have additional information or a separate site devoted to that seminar or workshop, include a link to the site.

◆ **Other seminar sites.** You will need a separate site (or separate sections of the same site) for each seminar you plan to present. Provide links to these sites both from within the main page and from the events calendar. Avoid promoting more than one seminar topic from within a single site (unless each seminar appears to be on its own site) to avoid confusing the visitor.

◆ **Office site.** Because seminar sites are so specialized, if you also intend to offer online client service or sales, you should keep these different functions separate. This can be done either by placing these functions on a separate Web site, with only a link and a brief explanation appearing on the seminar site, or by designing a single site that appears to be separate, a relatively simple task for a good designer.

Contract with a Webcasting Site

YOUR SEMINARS CAN REACH a larger audience and become even easier to attend if you broadcast them over the Internet. You don't even have to offer the seminar in front of a live audience (though you certainly can), and you save the cost of meeting rooms, snacks, and printed handouts. You can even store past seminars and allow people who were unable to attend your live seminar to attend an automated rebroadcast.

This is called Webcasting, and the latest innovations in technology make it surprisingly easy and affordable. Even though you can develop your own Webcasting capability by having your developer build this technology directly into your site, I don't recommend it. Webcasting a live seminar online requires some very specialized skills and a specialized Web site. In addition, the technology is both costly and rapidly changing. Thus, I recommend that you contract with an application service provider (ASP) specializing in online conferences and seminars. One of the best is Placeware Web Conferencing (http://www.placeware.com).

☞ **HELPFUL HINT:** One caution: Don't get too carried away with technology! Remember that most seminar participants or Web site visitors will be connecting at slow modem speeds, so avoid using options that require a large bandwidth (video, heavy use of graphics, etc.). On the other hand, don't be afraid to use this technology; simply use it in moderation. Be sure you always check your site from a computer with a slow modem.

An online seminar is very similar to a traditional seminar for the presenter. The only real difference is that you must do your presentation using a computer-generated slide show program such as Microsoft PowerPoint (standard overheads do not reside in a computer's memory, so there is nothing Placeware Web Conferencing can broadcast). The audio is provided through a streaming Web audio, via a 1-800 conference call, or both.

Unless your audiences all have access to high-bandwidth connections (cable, T1, satellite, etc.), avoid video conferences. Only a few ASPs support this, and it is costly. Plus, it will crash the computers of most prospects.

Placeware Web Conferencing provides full speaker training. Once you feel comfortable doing an online presentation with the software, take the time to test your presentation from a computer with a slow modem connection (work with your ASP to accomplish this—they have a vested interest in your presentation going smoothly). Strip out or modify anything that loads too slowly.

Placeware Web Conferencing also has a wide array of pricing options, depending on the level of support and number of seminars and conferences you intend to conduct. Like traditional hotels and conference centers, Placeware Web Conferencing offers a variety of room sizes to choose from for your seminar. The room accommodations range from ten to five hundred seats. Placeware also offers full meeting registration support as well as marketing, reminders, billing, etc. You can even have the ASP customize the look of its site to match your Web site (though unless seminars are the main method of marketing for you, this is probably not a cost-effective option). Decide what services you can provide yourself (you or your staff) and those that it would be more cost-effective for the ASP to handle. Then have the ASP price a number of options. Adjust the mix of services until you find a price you are comfortable with. For other Webcasting options, see "Building Specialized Niche Sites," Chapter 6, page 135.

◆ **Buy or lease a contact management system with automated e-mail capability.** As with the customer service-oriented site described earlier, you need the ability to track your e-mails as part of an integrated contact management system. For more contact

> ☞ **HELPFUL HINT:** There is extreme sensitivity to spamming (sending someone an unsolicited e-mail). Adverse reaction is much higher with e-mail than with regular mail. Many people consider an unwanted e-mail message an invasion of privacy. There can also be severe consequences to spamming (see Chapter 5 for more on spamming). DON'T SPAM!

management options, see Chapter 1 and "Staying in Touch with Your Clients" in Chapter 5.

◆ **Collect e-mail addresses for prospective seminar attendees from your current client base.** Obviously, to glean from your client list, you need to keep your e-mail address files current. See Chapter 1, page 15, for guidance on this process.

◆ **E-mail prospective seminar attendees obtained from list brokers.** Unlike more traditional mailings, e-mail lists are more difficult to obtain and must be used more carefully.

Thus, you must obtain your lists from an opt-in e-mail list broker. Such a list broker distributes e-mail addresses only for individuals who have specifically given their permission to be e-mailed about certain topics or offers if your use meets the release criteria. Here are some examples of such list brokers:

—BulletMail (http://www.bulletmail.com)

—Liszt (http://liszt.com)

—MatchLogic (http://www.matchlogic.com/index.asp)

—Netcreations (http://www.netcreations.com)

—PostMasterDirect.com (http://www.postmasterdirect.com)

—TargetPacks.com (http://www.targetpacks.com)

—24/7 Media (http://www.247media.com)

—yesmail.com (http://www.yesmail.com)

Some list brokers will provide you with the e-mail list names, while others require you to e-mail prospects through them. If you must e-mail through the list broker, it means that you will not be able to automate your e-mailings from your contact management system until the prospect responds. You will also find that typically no single list broker is going to have a large enough list of potential seminar attendees for your target prospects in your geographic area. That is why it is wise to order lists from multiple brokers and retain any e-mail addresses you do receive as part of your own opt-in e-mail list within your contact management system (see below).

Create Your Own Opt-in E-Mail Prospect List

OBTAIN POSTAL MAILING LISTS from traditional list brokers. Send out a "snail mail" letter promoting your online seminar (or series of seminars). This letter can directly promote a particular seminar, or it may simply ask recipients if they would like to be notified of upcoming future seminars. Ask in the letter for their e-mail address if they wish to be notified or are interested in more information on the seminars. By providing the e-mail address, they have opted in to your e-mail list. Retain their response for your files. You can now add them to your contact manager and include them in your seminar promotional e-mails.

Once you hold a few online seminars, you should begin receiving some e-mail referrals from your Web site (remember the referral section we created?). *Do not add these referrals directly to your opt-in e-mail list.* At this point the prospect has not opted in to your list. Instead, send out a special snail mail letter, introducing yourself and indicating that her name was referred to you as someone who might be interested in more information or in attending one of your seminars. As in the previous letter, ask for the e-mail address. If she responds, you can add her to your opt-in e-mail prospect list and include her in your seminar promotional e-mails.

Automatically Send Seminar Promotion E-Mails to Your Prospect List

ALWAYS PROVIDE AN E-MAIL reply link on all your e-mails that allows the client or prospect to opt out of receiving your seminar e-mails. If you don't provide this, you can be accused of spamming. For prospects who don't have an e-mail address or clients who prefer to be contacted by mail, have your contact manager notify you to send out the communications listed below via regular mail.

◆ **Send short teaser e-mails to build interest in the event.** These e-mails should ask penetrating questions of the prospect and then highlight a feature of the upcoming seminar that helps answer those questions. For example: "While college tuition has more than doubled since 1981, family income has risen only 22 percent. The average public four-year college charges over $8,000 a year for tuition, room, and board. Out-of-state college costs are now over $13,000, and private college over $21,000. If your child attended college today, could you afford it? What will the costs be in ten or fifteen years? To learn some practical college planning tips, attend the XYZ College Planning Seminar." Provide a link back to your Web site for more information. ASPs also offer this service for a fee, but I recommend that you do it yourself since this allows you to personalize the notes to your current clients.

◆ **Send an e-mail seminar brochure and registration link.** The seminar brochure and registration form reside on your Web site (and/or on the Placeware Web conferencing ASP site), so the e-mail is merely a short, enticing summary of the key points covered by the seminar, with a link back to the registration site. In order to participate in a Placeware Web conferencing event, the attendee must also create a personal "profile" on the Placeware Web conferencing site (usually via a link from your site). This profile includes basic address, contact information, a user name, and a password for security.

◆ **At the time of the seminar, send an e-mail reminder to all attendees** (if this is not already being done by the ASP) **with a link to the Webcast site**. Your e-mail should include brief instructions on how to access your seminar from the Webcast site.

Webcast Your Seminar

YOUR ATTENDEES WILL LOG ONTO the Webcast site (usually directly to Placeware Web conferencing, though you could provide a link from your site to the conferencing site). If already registered, the attendees click on "Attend an Event" (otherwise they register). They enter their e-mail addresses and conference passwords, then select your seminar from the list of events provided. This list will include more than just your events unless you have a customized version of the site. At this point a special browser loads on their computer.

The interaction during a Webcast is very similar to a live presentation. The white box on the left is where your presentation slides appear as you move through them on your computer. The attendees are free to go back over prior slides and catch up by clicking on the current slide. They hear you either through their phone or their computer. You can make highlights or comments on the slides as you speak. You can ask questions of your audience, and they can respond using a polling function. The attendees can also ask you questions, view a virtual seating chart, and communicate with each other during the presentation.

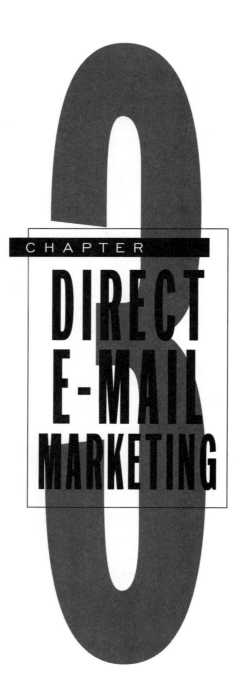

CHAPTER

DIRECT
E-MAIL
MARKETING

LET'S SAY YOU'RE CURRENTLY acquiring the bulk of your

new clients through a combination of direct mail and

cold calls, with some referrals to leaven the mix. You pur-

chase lists regularly and do a regular schedule of mail-

ings and phone calls each month. You and your staff

have a highly developed and efficient mailing and phone

follow-up system. From the contacts generated by this

system, you develop your new clients and a list of further

referrals. Your main goal is to put your name and ser-

vices in front of as many eyeballs as possible. You trust

that the products and services you offer and your charm-

ing personality will persuade a high percentage of these

contacts. In this case, you have a heavily *numbers-focused*

marketing strategy.

The Internet version of your current strategy would

use online technology to increase the reach of your marketing. Your focus here is to increase the number of potential clients exposed to your services. The principal online channels used in this strategy are a marketing-oriented business Web site, automated e-mail, and a contact management system. What follows are the steps necessary to develop this strategy.

Expand Your Marketing Area and Obtain Needed Licenses

UNLIKE TRADITIONAL MARKETING strategies, using the Web opens up the possibility of marketing over a much larger area—even on a regional or national basis. This is particularly true if you leverage your time well by using online virtual meetings or seminars. (See Chapter 1, "Customer Service," and Chapter 2, "Client Acquisition Seminars," for more details.) However, even if you plan to meet with prospects in person, the Web allows you to be much more efficient in finding prospects and scheduling appointments. Thus, since you plan to expand your market, you will need to obtain licenses for the larger region. These will require added cost and time that you need to incorporate into your planning.

Create a Web Site

FOR AN E-MAIL MARKETING STRATEGY, your site must, above all else, motivate the prospect to contact you. This means disturbing the clients, causing them to take some action. This can take the form of making them uncomfortable with their level of savings or planning. Alternatively, you can offer services or support they may not have currently.

Again, while you could have a generalist build your Web site, an understanding of the financial services marketplace is extremely helpful. Many of the marketing features you need are already fully developed on template sites. As explained before, the online compliance review speeds the site approval and updating process. (See Chapter 7, "Web Site Developers," for more information.)

Since your purpose here is to generate appointments, select content options for your site that are more than just *interesting*. No

> ☞ **HELPFUL HINT:** Any site that attempts to market a representative's services online must take time to reinforce the client-rep relationship. It is particularly important that you address the limitations of do-it-yourself online investing and why there is value in working with a professional adviser. If the prospect can see no real difference in the services he receives from you online and those of a discount broker, he will choose based on cost. You lose, every time!

matter how entertaining your site is, if clients don't contact you, it has failed! Your site should contain the following elements (these and other related topics are covered in much greater detail in "Content of a Typical Rep Site" on page 118 in Chapter 6): rep information, company or firm information, ability to refer a friend, and client account access and/or client trading (though this is less important with this type of site).

MAKE IT EASY FOR CLIENTS TO CONTACT YOU

THIS IS A CRITICAL FEATURE of an e-mail marketing site. You need to give prospects multiple opportunities and multiple methods by which they can contact you. Along with being part of the Contact Me section of your site, your e-mail link should appear in as many locations throughout your site as possible. This includes embedding it in the text of your bio, articles, newsletters, and at the bottom of most HTML pages. In addition, be sure to offer value-added services on your site that require the person to send an e-mail or complete the Contact Me section (for instance, a free initial portfolio review). Also, be sure your phone and fax numbers appear often throughout the site.

INTERACTIVE APPOINTMENT CALENDAR

ONE OF THE BEST WAYS that a Web site can benefit an e-mail marketing campaign is to provide a means for a prospect to self-schedule an appointment. The links from your e-mails can even go directly to this section of your site. By posting and regularly updating your calendar and allowing prospects to schedule appointments online you save yourself, your staff, and your prospect time and effort. This is also an opportunity to collect some basic demographic and address information.

This function can either be a part of the template site or it can be a stand-alone site with links to the template site. Which you choose will depend upon your contact management system and the amount of functionality you want within the appointment calendar. Ideally, this calendar should tie directly into your contact management system so that when an appointment is entered online, it is also entered into your contact management system. The other option is to have an e-mail sent to you each time the calendar is updated. In either case, you should always send an e-mail confirmation for any appointments set up in this manner.

Financial planning tools, market data information, and other interactive functions are all possibilities; however, with an e-mail marketing site, you are less interested in having prospects interact with your site than you are in moving them to action. This means you must choose online tools and calculators that expose potential gaps in their planning. An example might be a calculator that shows the impact of compound interest and cost of procrastination. Online financial planning tools are useful here since they can highlight needs. Avoid tools that provide or suggest solutions online. In every case, choose tools and calculators that motivate the prospect to contact you.

LIFE, ANNUITY, AND/OR MUTUAL FUND INFORMATION

LIMIT THE AMOUNT of specific product information you provide on this type of site. Provide general information on the types and brands of insurance or funds that you offer. Avoid links to the sponsor's site. If you provide all the prospect's product answers on the site, they have less reason to contact you.

NEWSLETTERS AND ARTICLES

ONLINE PUBLICATIONS CAN BE a powerful tool for an e-mail marketing site. Remember that most visitors to this type of site will be prospects. Thus, they have no real understanding of what you do.

Include articles that emphasize the professional planning services that you provide. Give specific examples of the types of services you offer (portfolio analysis, estate planning, retirement planning, asset management, college planning, business planning, etc.). Develop fictitious examples that will help you illustrate the steps in your planning process.

Another approach is to include respected third-party articles that reinforce the need for the type of services you offer or give examples of situations caused by poor planning. Be selective. Avoid generic articles prepared by third parties since these are rarely specific enough for your purposes.

As with the client acquisition seminar, you will need to do the following (see Chapter 2 for more details):

◆ Buy or lease a contact management system with automated e-mail capability.

◆ E-mail potential prospects obtained from list brokers. Use the opt-in e-mail list described in Chapter 2.

◆ Create your own opt-in e-mail prospect list based on a consolidated database you create from e-mail opt-in lists, responses to direct mailings, clients, and referrals (no spamming!). Several of the best traditional list brokers are the American List Counsel (http://www.amlist.com), FindMoreBuyers.com (http://www.findmorebuyers.com/index.cfm), and USADATA (http://www.usadata.com). Although you can't e-mail from their lists, you can send regular mailings and request the prospects' e-mail addresses. By the way, the first two sites also include an excellent library of direct mail techniques and tips, many of which are adaptable to e-mail marketing.

◆ FindMoreBuyers.com also offers a database marketing approach in which you provide them with the top 20 percent of your clients. They then use an extensive database to match your client's demographic and psychographic profiles with other prospects. This becomes your new list. Another good site for tips on direct marketing is Sales & Marketing Executives Marketing Library (http://www.marketinglibrary.com/sme-fr5-directmail.htm).

◆ Obtain missing e-mail addresses through online e-mail look-up directories.

AUTOMATIC E-MAILS

AUTOMATICALLY SEND OUT A regular schedule of marketing e-mails to your list. Remember to avoid spamming by always providing an opt-out e-mail reply link.

Take Time to Plan Your E-Mail Design, Content, and Timing

YOUR E-MAILS, LIKE YOUR regular mailings, are an extension of yourself. Your prospect's first impression of you is likely to come from your e-mails and regular mailings.

There are a number of ways to structure your communications with prospects. Some of these I've discussed in earlier strategies, including personal e-mails to celebrate events, e-mail newsletter links, portfolio review e-mails, and teaser e-mails to build interest in the events. We've also discussed Web sites, online meetings, and seminars. Most of these can be adapted, with a few modifications, to this strategy of direct e-mail marketing. However, the one method that is the most directly applicable is the e-mail marketing letter. Here are some guidelines for developing a good e-mail marketing letter.

DESIGN

ANY E-MAIL YOU SEND to a prospect should be fully integrated with your regular direct mail campaign. Don't be spontaneous! There is a time and a place for spontaneity—this isn't it! Also, don't reinvent the wheel here. You have a certain look and feel to your existing marketing materials, so don't make your new e-mail materials dramatically different.

Yes, I know that e-mail can do some really cool things (animation, color graphics, banner links, splash pages, and so on). But just because it is possible doesn't mean you should do it. If you have been online for any length of time, you know that the number of e-mails you receive has skyrocketed (even when you eliminate the spammers). E-mail clutter is becoming an increasingly significant problem.

Studies show that nearly half of all consumers say they're more likely to respond to e-mail if they've already seen a print ad or mailing from the same company.[1] There are some very good reasons for this; there are a lot of e-mail scams out there. Familiarity lends credibility to your e-mails, and this helps get your messages noticed. Remember also that not all e-mail services are created equal. In other words, just because your e-mail service allows animation doesn't mean that your customer's e-mail does. It may look great when you send it but read like hieroglyphics when your prospect opens it.

Finally, most e-mail programs allow you to change the font style, size, and color, as well as add background graphics and even sound. While this kind of formatting can make an e-mail look good, it can also easily become distracting and actually undermine your communication. In this case, less is more. Your e-mail should stand out based on its content, not its formatting. Pick an easy-to-read font, and stay consistent with type size and style. Try not to use bold or underline. Don't use all caps—it's the e-mail equivalent of shouting.

CONTENT

CONTENT IS KING. The content of your e-mail is critical and should be developed like any good marketing letter. Resist the tendency to dash off an e-mail just to stay in communication. Bad communication is still bad, no matter how frequently it's sent.

Here are some tips for writing good business e-mail:

◆ **Choose the words for the subject line of the e-mail with care.** In many cases the recipients will determine whether to read the rest of your e-mail from these few words. The subject should tell the readers what your message is about. Don't try to trick or tease them into reading further, because it is too easy to hit the delete key.

◆ **Keep to a single subject.** If you combine several subjects in one e-mail, at least one of those concepts is going to get lost. You can introduce several ideas—just don't change subjects. This is what to avoid: "Now that I've explained our exciting new financial planning service, let me tell you about the new mutual fund that XYZ recently introduced."

◆ **Identify yourself clearly.** Remember your real purpose is to motivate someone to contact you (directly or through your site).

Accomplish that, and your e-mail has done its job. To do this, you need to make the recipient understand the five Ws (not necessarily in this order):

1 Who you are
2 What action you want them to take
3 When they need to take that action (if you don't tell them to call now, don't assume they will)
4 Where you are located and your contact information
5 Why you wrote the e-mail

Of the five Ws, number five is the most challenging.

Write your content from the perspective of your audience.[2] What are your clients looking for? Do they want to gain any of these?

—Health
—Popularity
—Time
—Comfort
—Money
—Leisure
—Praise from others
—Self-confidence
—Security in life
—Personal prestige

Or, do they want to
—Satisfy their curiosity
—Win others' affection
—Acquire or collect things
—Improve themselves
—Express themselves

Does your audience want to avoid
—Worry
—Embarrassment
—Doubts
—Expenditure of time
—Risks and threats

Or, maybe they want to be
—Creative
—Efficient
—Up-to-date
—Sociable
—Good parents
—Influential
—Recognized
—Proud
—First among their friends

Obviously no single message can or should touch on all these wants. In fact, a financial service message probably doesn't relate directly to a number of these desires. However, even when a want seems unrelated, it may influence prospects' financial decisions. While these nonfinancial goals are more difficult to work into a good marketing e-mail, they can be very compelling if used effectively.

In writing a persuasive message, you need to select a few key wants that are drivers among your target audience. That is, the importance of the want is sufficient to motivate most of your audience to take action. The company MarketResearch.com (http://www.marketresearch.com) offers a Web site with thousands of research reports that profile the interests and preferences of a wide range of potential target audiences.

Once you isolate what your particular audience is looking for, examine the products and services you offer. Now, for each want, answer this question: If your target audience were to use your products and services effectively, how would this key want be fulfilled? Make sure you can establish a strong logical connection between the services you offer and the key want. If you can't make a strong case, eliminate that want. No matter how terrific a planner you are, you don't want to promise what you can't accomplish. Write down the logical connections that you used for each of the remaining key wants. I'll explain why in a minute.

> ☞ **HELPFUL HINT:** Make your e-mail as easy to read as possible. Don't assume your prospect is familiar with the subject of your e-mail. This is an easy trap to fall into. Just because you understand what *portfolio analysis* means, don't take for granted that your prospect has a clue. Pretend you are describing the subject to your grandmother. How would you make her understand? Put the draft of your e-mail aside and reread it the next day. How easy is it to grasp? If you stumble at all in rereading it, it needs revision.

Response to Mailings

Type of Merchandise	Jan	Feb	Mar	Apr	May	Jun	Jul	Aug	Sep	Oct	Nov	Dec
General Consumer	EX	FR	GD	GD	PR	PR	PR	GD	EX	EX	EX	GD
Business Merchandise	EX	EX	GD	GD	FR	FR	PR	PR	EX	EX	GD	PR
Business Sales Lead	GD	EX	EX	GD	FR	PR	PR	PR	EX	EX	GD	PR
Financial Services	GD	FR	GD	FR	PR	PR	PR	GD	EX	EX	GD	PR
Produce Store Traffic	EX	GD	FR	EX	GD	PR	PR	GD	EX	GD	EX	GD

EX = Excellent   GD = Good   FR = Fair   PR = Poor

SOURCE: BY, AND COMPLIMENTS OF, AMERICAN LIST COUNSEL, 1996.

Now, restate the prospect's wants in the form of a question or a challenge. As you construct these questions and challenges, be sure your purpose is always to intrigue and motivate the prospect to contact you—avoid promissory statements. Keep your questions or challenges short (one line if possible), pointed (don't mince words), and believable (avoid sweeping generalities). These restated key wants make up the fifth W (why you wrote the e-mail). This, in turn, becomes the core message of your e-mail. Now make sure your e-mail includes the other four Ws—and always give your prospect an embedded link back to your Web site in the e-mail.

Your letter should be no more than two or three paragraphs. Brevity is particularly important with an e-mail since so few lines appear in the review screen of most browsers. If all your great ideas won't fit, save them, because you're going to be e-mailing prospects again next month. This will help keep your e-mails fresh and different.

Be sure your compliance department reviews your planned e-mails. Remember, this is sales literature.

Now use the list of logical connections you made earlier to develop your respondent sales track. You need to know exactly what you (or your staff) are going to say to reinforce your sales message. Notice that I'm asking you to develop your sales track based on *how your products and services fulfill your prospects' wants and needs.* At this point, prospects really don't care how wonderful you think your services are or how well your product has performed. They want to know how your products and services help achieve what is important to them!

TIMING

AS YOU CAN SEE from the table above, certain times of the year are better for financial services mailings than others. These same factors hold true for e-mails as well.

Remember that one or two e-mails does not a campaign make! If you expect results, you must be persistent and consistent. Something should be going out to your entire prospect database at least monthly. Alternate regular mailings with e-mails, allowing the channels to complement and reinforce each other. Plan to do phone follow-up and/or a personal e-mail to any respondent.

CHAPTER

NICHE MARKETING

4

NICHE MARKETING MEANS selecting a portion of your potential market and focusing all your marketing efforts on that narrower segment. This method goes well beyond targeting a few mailings or e-mails toward the wants of some portion of your database (as described in the previous chapter). Niche marketing is a complete change in business focus. You actually give up marketing to a large number of potential prospects so that you can free up time to more aggressively pursue your selected niche. This isn't easy and requires a great deal of discipline on your part. Some of you are already doing this; others are looking to move into a niche.

Let's begin with the basics. What constitutes a niche? Actually, your marketplace can be divided into a virtually infinite number of niches. These niches can be based on demographics (age, sex, marital status, ethnicity, etc.), geography (city, county, state), education, income, industry, employer, union membership, professional affiliation, association membership, religious affiliation, and so on—the list goes on endlessly. An excellent reference on developing a niche market is Steve Moeller's audio-book *Effort-Less Marketing for Financial Advisors.* Steve offers a list of the top twenty-two niche markets for advisers. While certainly not an exhaustive list, this should provide you with some excellent ideas for developing your own niches. Regardless of which niche you choose, your choice should be based on these key factors:

◆ **The potential segment size.** How many prospects are available? Too few and it's not worth the effort.

◆ **Market saturation.** How many competitors do you face?

◆ **Disposable income.** Does the niche have enough spendable income?

◆ **Your affinity with the market.** Do you have some shared background, experience, or heritage in common?

◆ **Barriers to entry.** Are there any added costs to reach this market? What background do you need to work this market? Too many barriers and it may not be worth your time and/or money. Too few, and competitors can quickly imitate your success.

Finding Niche Marketing Support Online

AMONG THE MOST USEFUL functions of the Internet in facilitating niche marketing is its ability to provide you with background information on a niche. There is a surprisingly large amount of information available online regarding even some very obscure market niches.

To find this information you need to be able to effectively search the Internet. The first step is to know where to look. The portion of Appendix B, "Major Search Engines and Directories," is a good place to start. However, searching the Internet is more than simply entering a few keywords in a search engine or directory.

Second, even if you choose the correct keywords, no search engine searches the entire Web. In February 2000, a joint study published by Inktomi and the NEC Research Institute estimated that there were 1 billion indexable pages on the Web. Even the most comprehensive search engine reaches only about 60 percent of this total, and many search engines reach as little as 10 percent. However, some of the search engines or directories that reach a more limited portion of the Internet have more intelligent indexes. Thus, you get more meaningful results. There is nothing more frustrating and useless than to get 200,000 search responses *in no particular order.* Therefore, plan to search for your information on more than one search engine.

Third, give some thought to what keywords you plan to search with. Think about which words are unique to a particular niche—the more unique the better. Most search engines allow you to restrict your search. This is a very useful feature. If the search allows Boolean logic (use of the words *and, or, if, then, else, not*), string your keywords together with the appropriate operator. Many search engines will allow you to do a new keyword search within the results of your earlier search. You can rapidly focus your search this way. When you get your results back, look for any sites that are related to your niche topic (even if not closely related). Use these to expand your list of keywords. After you do your initial search, change the order of the words in your search (this can have a dramatic impact on the results).

Most of all, don't give up! This will take time, and it will be frustrating. However, the payoff can be dramatic. You may stumble across an association focused on your niche market, or a chat room devoted to prospects from your niche. Even when the site itself isn't particularly useful, you may find links to other sites or offline contact information you can follow up by phone or mail. The amount of information you can find this way can save you years of traditional research time. In addition, as you learn more about your niche market, you can better target your searches. So go back and search again after you've done your initial research. (See "How do I use search services?" in the "Passive Prospecting" section of Chapter 5 for more information on search engines and directories.)

Following are a few examples of the type of niche marketing information available online and the kind of online support services available for niche marketing. Don't forget that many of the general marketing ideas and techniques discussed in the preceding three chapters can also be adapted to niche marketing. In such cases, I'll refer you to the appropriate earlier chapter. Thus, the focus in these next examples is on *other* support services or marketing techniques where the Internet can specifically assist in niche marketing. Although the general action steps are basically the same for each of the four segments, you need to apply them in somewhat different ways to properly target each niche.

Job-Site or Benefits Marketing

LET'S SAY YOU'VE DEVELOPED some expertise in marketing to small and midsize businesses and their employees. Most of your income comes from employee pension planning and collateral sales. Thus, your current marketing strategy is based on *group sales* and *job-site marketing*.

Online support for this strategy includes accessing sources of market information or potential prospects and providing easier access to employees. This strategy is two-pronged. You must be on the lookout for new companies to build your employer-client base, and you must sell and service each company's employees in an efficient manner. The principal online channels used in this strategy are search engines/directories, specialized business Web sites, e-mail, Webcasting services, and a contact management system. Here are the steps necessary to develop this strategy:

PERFORM INTERNET SEARCHES LOOKING FOR USEFUL SITES

THE RESULTS OF YOUR searches will, of course, vary depending on when you do the search, as well as the keywords used and search engines chosen. Here is an unscientific, and certainly not exhaustive, sampling of the types of useful Web sites that result from one day of this kind of search. Keywords were *benefits, plan administrator, administration, 401k, 403b, pension, chat room, job-site marketing, work-site marketing,* and *layoffs.*

◆ **401(k) information.** The 401kHelpCenter.com (http://www.401khelpcenter.com) provides educational information for plan sponsors, small businesses, and employees, but you can use this information yourself. The Center for Due Diligence

☞ **HELPFUL HINT:** Do your due diligence! Just because you found an online vendor that seems to fit your needs or provides you with very useful information doesn't mean that its information is correct or that it is a legitimate business. That applies to the online vendors cited in this book as well as those you find yourself—I've done my best to list only legitimate firms, but I can't guarantee them. Look at the credentials of the site authors. Do they have the experience and training necessary to give weight to their information? Find out if there is a sponsoring organization or owner that might bias their information. Check their business background and their credit reports with Dun & Bradstreet (http://www.dnb.com). Check with the Better Business Bureau (http://www.bbb.org) to see if any complaints have been filed against them. Finally, check with your compliance department.

(http://401kduediligence.com), however, was designed specifically for your use. It is an independent consulting/research organization specializing exclusively in full-service 401(k) program competitive analysis for financial service professionals (your broker-dealer may even offer a discount on its services). Both Search401k.com (http://www.search401k.com) and 401kexchange.com (http://www.401kexchange.com) are also structured for the adviser and offer free service to assist in the search and selection process.

◆ **403(b)/TSA information.** The 403(b)/TSA Information Center (http://403bwise.com) provides educational information for those interested in plan development or administration. The site has an excellent chat room.

◆ **Benefits attorneys.** It can be difficult to find a local attorney who specializes in employee benefits. With the Internet, you are no longer limited to the local area. There are a number of benefit attorneys with sites online. One of the better sites is http://benefits attorney.com.

◆ **Employee benefits research.** The Employee Benefits Research Institute (http://www.ebri.org) has a wealth of current research and policy studies. Another similar site is freeERISA.com (http://www.freeerisa.com).

◆ **Employee benefits sites.** Benefitslink.com (http://www.benefits link.com), PlanSponsor.com (http://www.plansponsor.com), International Foundation of Employee Benefit Plans (http://www.ifebp.org), and Benefitnews.com (http://www.benefit news.com) are all sites for employee benefits managers, but they are equally useful to advisers. These sites allow you to keep up with the concerns of the very people to whom you are trying to sell your products. Pay particular attention to the chat rooms.

◆ **Employee chat rooms.** Here is an article from the November 1999 issue of *Plan Sponsor* magazine on the development of employee chat rooms to discuss problems with employer pension programs—including links to those chat rooms: (http://www.asset pub.com/psnov99/nov99PS020.html). This kind of information can be extremely useful, but follow up quickly since news articles don't stay posted indefinitely.

◆ **Layoffs.** The reason for including the HRLive site (http://www.hrlive.com) may not be immediately apparent since it is actually for use by human resource professionals. However, by using the site's "Layoff Update," you can identify all the layoffs that have occurred anywhere in the United States over the last year. You can approach these companies by offering to conduct seminars for departing employees to help them understand their options for protecting their retirement funds.

◆ **Pension administration.** A number of different kinds of pension administration sites have surfaced. Administrators from offices of varying sizes and from many locations are willing to work with reps, such as Blaze SSI (http://www.blazessi.com) or Benefits Management, Inc. (http://net2.netacc.net/~bmgt). There are quite a few such firms should you choose to work with one, but remember that just because they have a site does not mean they do quality work—do your due diligence. If you would rather offer the pension administration yourself, the Advisors 401(k) site (http://www.advi sors-401k.com) should interest you. This site offers 401(k) pension administration software designed to be used by advisers. The third type of site offers 401(k) software that the company can use to develop a do-it-yourself plan. Such a program is 401(k) Easy (http://401keasy.com). This may be of interest if you don't target that portion of the benefits market and simply want to offer assistance to the firm in setting up such a program.

◆ **Section 125 sites.** Benefit Innovations, Inc. (http://www. benefitinnovations.com) is a company that specializes in self-administered flexible benefit and cafeteria plans. Though there is no direct compensation for you, you can introduce your client to this company as a nice value-added service and open the door to discussions about section-125-qualified products that you do offer.

◆ **Seminars.** I ran across a new seminar system offered by Emerald Publications called Worksite Direct (http://www.emerald publications.com/sems/newSeminars3.htm). This system can be presented as a public seminar, as a private one-on-one discussion with clients, or in a cosponsored environment.

◆ **Competitors.** Finally, it is always useful to see what your competitors are doing. Obviously, if you know a local competitor's name, you can look specifically for the site. However, of even more use is to find out what small and large competitors in different areas are doing or saying on their sites. Here are a few examples: Quicken Team Vest (http://www.teamvest.com/quick/), Wall Street Access Advisory Services (http://advisor.wsaccess.com), Raymond J. Luca (http://www.rjlinc.com/index.html), Capital Benefits (http://yourwealth.com/index.htm), and Pine Lake Advisors, Inc. (http://pinelakeadvisors.com). Use these sites to focus your own marketing or revise the look and functionality of your Web site.

CREATE WEB SITES

FOR THIS BENEFITS STRATEGY, you need two different types of Web sites. First, you need a single site for employer information and multiple sites for employee information (the other option would be to develop everything on a single custom site with multiple segments). The employer site's purpose is to explain who you are, what your experience is, and which types of services you offer.

The employee sites' purpose is to provide benefits information customized by company and to describe your additional services. The potential complexity of these types of sites requires developers with specialized knowledge of our industry.

◆ **The employer site.** This is your primary marketing site. The site will require content geared to a business-to-business structure (rather than the typical rep Web site business-to-consumer structure). This means you need to alter the way you write your descriptions. Businesses are more interested in a factual versus an emotional appeal. They are also less impressed with calculators and interactive functions. Basically, they want you to cut to the chase.

Company information. Include a complete description of your firm. If possible, include one or more of the following: your mission statement, area of specialization, financials, Better Business Bureau membership/seal, Dun & Bradstreet credit rating, and description of your broker-dealer (with a link to the broker-dealer's home page). You also need a bio highlighting your and your staff's job-site benefits marketing experience and any specialized expertise. This section should be more elaborate than what is written for a typical template site since businesses are typically more demanding. You also need to have a list of your licenses, where you are approved to do business, and any professional designations you have acquired. If you have any business testimonials from key corporate managers or officers, be sure to include them. Business clients expect this, and they expect to have contact information included, so be sure you clear this thoroughly with your business clients in advance. You should include an online map to your office(s).

Referral. In addition to being more formal and including business reply information, you should ask for referrals online, just as with earlier strategies.

Contact me. This section should be an online form rather than a simple e-mail. This is more professional looking and allows you to ask for more information, such as title, business name, business address, phone and extension, fax, business e-mail (it might be different from the address being used to access your site), etc. You can also provide fields that allow the business prospect to specify an area of interest.

Interactive appointment calendar. This is similar to the function described in the e-mail marketing campaign in Chapter 3. It allows the business prospect to self-schedule an appointment.

Newsletters and articles. A benefits newsletter is a useful selling tool, if you keep it current and relevant to the business. The same can be said for third-party articles. In either case, the employer is looking to see how he can increase retention, lower his human resources costs, or make his fringe benefits package more competitive without dramatically increasing his overhead. Although showing the employer how to improve employees' financial planning efforts or retirement income is of interest, the preceding issues are usually the drivers.

◆ **The employee sites.** These sites will be very similar in structure to the customer-service-strategy site described in Chapter 1; thus most of the site functions apply to these employee sites as well. The major differences are highlighted below:

Site layout variations. You will have a single template layout with passwords that limit the employees' access to Web pages with their employer's content. Thus, each company's employees will see only the content for their company. This allows you to adjust your content to reflect the differences between company benefit programs. It also lets you customize your sales promotions and service visits to fit the calendars of the different companies.

Customization to match the company site. One of the options you can offer to the employer is a unique site that matches the company intranet site's look and feel, making navigation for the employee much easier. Caution: This is an option that shouldn't be oversold. It should be reserved for larger employers; otherwise, it will get too expensive to be cost-effective. In addition, some employers want a clear separation between the company's sponsored site and your benefits site.

Company benefits section. Each site will include a description of benefits offered to employees as a result of your agreement with each employer. You can offer to include descriptions of other company benefits as well, should the company wish. Since you will be offering 401(k) plan administration, you can also take requests for additional plan information and respond through this site. Eventually (though no vendor currently offers this option), you might integrate your software-reporting function to post an employee's specific information online, based on password access to your administration software.

AUTOMATICALLY SEND MARKETING E-MAILS TO YOUR OPT-IN BUSINESS AND EMPLOYEE E-MAIL LISTS

CONSTRUCT YOUR EMPLOYER e-mail list in the same manner discussed in Chapter 3, "Direct E-mail Marketing." Be sure you actively solicit employee e-mail addresses for both work and home from the employer and the employee. This can be done with a simple memo from the company to all employees requesting this information.

TAKE TIME TO PLAN YOUR E-MAIL DESIGN, CONTENT, AND TIMING

JUST AS WITH DIRECT E-MAIL marketing, you need to construct a program of marketing e-mails. The difference is that you will need to develop two campaigns. The first is to recruit new company clients, and the second is to promote products to and provide service for the employees of the companies. You will also need to promote your actual and virtual job-site meetings as part of both programs.

WEBCAST YOUR EMPLOYEE SEMINARS

PROVIDE A LINK TO A Webcasting site to facilitate virtual job-site meetings, similar to the seminars discussed in Chapter 2. This will reduce the amount of time needed during work hours for employee group meetings.

Senior Market Sales

YOU'VE FOCUSED YOUR practice on the mature Americans who possess 77 percent of all financial assets.[1] Most of your income comes from estate planning, benefits distribution, and collateral sales. Thus, your current marketing strategy is based on age.

As with other niche markets, this strategy can use online support to more efficiently access market information, locate potential prospects, and market to these prospects. The principal online channels used in this strategy are search engines/directories, a specialized business Web site, e-mail, and a contact management system. Here are the steps necessary to develop this strategy:

PERFORM AN INTERNET SEARCH FOR RELEVANT SITES

HERE IS A SAMPLING of the types of Web sites that resulted from one day of searching. Keywords were *retirement, retirement planning, estate planning, retired senior mature, mature market, senior market,* and *retirement planning adviser.*

There are many articles available online that can help you better understand the senior market and its needs. The Internet is an excellent way to come up to speed or update yourself on this market (remember that articles have a relatively short shelf life, so print them as you find them). Here are a few examples of some that I came across: "The Forgotten Generation? Targeting the Senior Market Online," from *Ad/Insight,* 1999 (http://www.channel seven.com/adinsight/commentary/1999comm/comm19991013. shtml), "Life Stages of the Mature Market," from *American Demographics,* 1996 (http://www.demographics.com/publications /ad/96_ad/9609_ad/9609af02.htm), "USADATA.com Consultant Reports—Demographics and Markets—Older American Information Directory" (http://dtq.usadata.com/consultant/ detail_access.asp?datasource=ska&id=GH64). This is an excellent general source for all sorts of information on niche markets under http://www.usadata.com and the "Data to Go" link. However, all data is fee-based.

◆ **Consultants.** I found an advertising consulting firm that specializes in marketing to the fifty-plus population. The firm offers online consultation for both direct mail and advertising. It also offers a free online education program. Check Evergreen Advertising and Marketing (http://www.eamnet.com).

◆ **Estate planning attorneys.** A number of attorneys specialize in estate planning, and the Web is an excellent tool for finding them. Here are two good examples: Charles A. Tingle Jr., P.C. (http://tingleatlaw.home.mindspring.com), and the Law Offices of Paul Cheverton (http://www.wealthtransfers.com/index.html).

◆ **Prospect/client publications and calendars.** American Custom Publishing Corporation is a custom printer of newsletters, brochures, calendars, and even "slide-guide" reference booklets specifically for the over-fifty market (http://www.acpinc.com). I also found a firm, the Practice Development Institute, that specializes in niche newsletters, one on estate planning (other topics included employee benefits, family business, financial planning, and health care) (http://www.pdiglobal.com/estate2.html).

◆ **Publications.** Senior Market Advisor Online is a publication specializing in providing marketing information to agents and planners who sell to the mature market (http://www.seniormarketadvisor.com). I also found a publication that specializes in providing technical information about estate planning, trust fund administration, and investing assets for financial planning and building wealth: Trust and Estates Online (http://www.trustsandestates.com).

◆ **Sites for seniors.** A large number of excellent sites are devoted to the needs of seniors. These can be a good way to begin understanding their concerns. Two examples are Age Venture News Service (http://www.demko.com) and AARP (http://www.aarp.org). Of particular interest are the sections on technology and the research section.

◆ **Competitors.** Here are a few examples of competitor sites of varying sizes that focus on the senior market: Elder Planning Advisors (http://www.elderplanningadvisors.com), Estate Planning Supersite (http://www.estateplanbasics.com), and Gilman & Ciocia (http://runningman.com/centerforestateplan).

PRODUCE A GOOD WEB SITE

FOR A SENIOR MARKET STRATEGY, the content of the Web site is very similar to what I suggested in Chapter 1 for the *customer service* market strategy. Although the primary purpose of the senior-market Web site is sales and service, it does require a different environment than the customer service site. Seniors, one of the most rapidly growing Internet segments, are looking for something different from the typical customer. The mature client wants an online environment that is easy to use and feels comfortable.

Here are some suggestions. Make sure your site is extremely easy to understand and to navigate. Avoid confusing graphics, splash screens, or special Java scripts. Be sure your site's content is relevant, useful, and nonthreatening. Add special sections devoted to activities and news of interest to seniors (search the Web to get ideas for these sections). Expand the event calendar to include community events for seniors. Change and update these frequently. Provide links to sites of interest to seniors. Sponsor a chat room on your site. Before your site goes live, have individuals in your target age range test your site, and listen carefully to their suggestions.

The design and content suggestions above are not something a template site can easily accommodate, so a template site is not recommended in this case. Template sites also may be limited in the selection of fonts and font sizes and in many cases do not provide for users with physical disabilities. The design of a mature-market site needs to allow for users with some visual, hearing, or other physical impairment. For more information, check out the latest version of the Web Content Accessibility Guidelines (http://www.w3.org/TR/1999/WAI-WEBCONTENT-19990505/).

SET UP YOUR CONTACT MANAGEMENT SYSTEM TO AUTOMATICALLY SEND OUT MARKETING E-MAILS TO YOUR OPT-IN LIST
CONSTRUCT YOUR E-MAIL list as discussed in Chapter 3, "Direct E-mail Marketing."

COORDINATE YOUR E-MAIL DESIGN, CONTENT, AND TIMING
JUST AS WITH direct e-mail marketing, you need to construct a program of marketing e-mails.

High-Net-Worth Marketing

YOUR TARGET IS THE WEALTHY. Most of your income comes from very targeted estate planning, endowments, financial planning, tax planning, and personal services to those with high net worth. Thus, your current marketing strategy is based on *expertise, service,* and *image.*

The high-net-worth marketing strategy uses online support to more efficiently access market information, locate potential prospects, and offer more personalized service. The principal online channels used in this strategy are search engines/directories, a specialized Web site, e-mail, Webcasting services, and a contact management system. Here are the steps necessary to develop this strategy:

DO AN INTERNET SEARCH LOOKING FOR USEFUL SITES

HERE IS A SAMPLING of Web sites that resulted from one day of searching; again, this is not an exhaustive list. I'm sure that with a little work, you can do even better. Keywords included *high net worth market, high net worth adviser, wealth management, exclusive by invitation select, HNW,* and *affluent.*

◆ **Articles on the high-net-worth market.** There are a large number of articles on this subject online. The Fidelity Advisor Institute has a number of educational articles, but the FAI Retirement Package is the most relevant (http://fiis.fidelity.com/fai) and includes several articles. Deloitte & Touche annually publish "Tips for High-Income, High-Net-Worth Individuals." The 2001 edition includes twenty-one tips (http://www.dtonline.com/taxguide2000/high1.htm).

Another good background article is from a 2001 issue of *Fortune,* "Managing Your Wealth" (http://www.fortune.com/fortune/sections/financial.htm). This article is written from the perspective of high-net- worth clients and discusses why they need the experience of a financial adviser. A good article on dealing with high-net-worth business owners is "Succession Planning and Exit Strategies for the High-Net-Worth Business Owner," *CPA Journal* (http://www.nysscpa.org/cpajournal/1999/0999/features/f30999.htm). "Lifetime Settlements—A Resource for Your High-Net-Worth Clients," a 1998 article in *Financial Services Journal Online* (http://fsc.fsonline.com/fsj/archive/050198mang.html), is the first of a three-part article on lifetime settlements discussing the sale of an in-force life insurance policy to a third party.

◆ **Consultants.** I located a research firm that offers targeted services for the high-net-worth market: Rainier Group (http://www.rainiergroup.com/institu/). The company develops your firm's marketing plan, trains your staff or your salespeople on the unique needs of this market, and provides ongoing marketing and customer service support. A firm with a slightly different twist is HNW Digital (http://www.worthinteractive.com). This firm sponsors several sites that cater to the needs of HNW individuals as well as providing marketing support to those that market to this group.

◆ **Mailing Lists.** This was an interesting find. Here is a site that will sell you lists targeted exclusively to the wealthy: Who$Wealthy.com (http://www.whosewealthy.net/). In addition to a general list of 2.2 million names, the company sells targeted lists of wealthy stock investors, pentamillionaires (at least $5 million), corporate directors, and so on.

◆ **Product sponsors.** A large number of financial products and services designed specifically for sale to the high-net-worth market are promoted online. These offerings can be very helpful in locating products and services that meet the unique needs of this market. However, make sure you check with your broker-dealer, because you can only sell products for which you are licensed and that have been approved in advance by your broker-dealer.

◆ **Publications.** In my searches I came across an online publication, *Private Asset Management* (http://www.iiwealthmanagement.com), that is updated daily; it focuses exclusively on marketing investment-management, financial, and advisory services to the high-net-worth arena. I also found an excellent three-book series: *Cultivating the Affluent: How to Segment and Service the High-Net-Worth Market; Cultivating the Affluent II: Leveraging High-Net-Worth Client and Advisor Relationships;* and *Private Wealth—Insight*

☞ **HELPFUL HINT:** Be sure you search the Net periodically to update your articles. Online articles are being written daily. Thus, you never know when a particularly good article will appear. Plan to do an article search once a month just to see what's new. Also, be sure to look for publication dates. Sometimes "new" articles are actually old articles being republished on a new site. Most information becomes dated after three or four years (and technical information in as little as six months).

into the High-Net-Worth Market, all by Russ Alan Prince and Karen Maru File. Russ also has a new book: *eWealth: Understanding the Internet Millionaire.* The four books are available through *Institutional Investor Newsletters'* iihighnetworth.com (http://www.iihigh networth.com).

◆ **Sites for high-net-worth individuals.** There are many such sites, and all of them provide you with opportunities (you are probably aware of quite a few brick-and-mortar companies that cater to the wealthy—most of these now have a Web site). Some allow advertising on their site and an opportunity to promote your services. Even where that isn't possible, providing a link to these sites from your Web site is a service for wealthy prospects and customers. Some examples of these kinds of sites are RRCM.com's Millionaire Village, a shopping mall for millionaires (http://www.millionaire village.com/index.htm); EHedge.com, a family of hedge funds (http://www.rrcm.com); and Sothebys.com (http://www. sothebys.com/), YachtWorld.com (http://www.yachtworld.com), CEO.com (http://ceo.com), Neiman Marcus (http://www. neimanmarcus.com), and Aircraft Dealer Online (http://www. aircraftdealer.com).

◆ **Competitors.** It is always a good idea to see what your large and small competitors in this market niche are doing. Here is a sampling: Oxford Group LTD (http://www.ofac.com), Capital Resource Advisors (http://www.cradv.com), Estate Street Partners LLC (http://www.taxdeferrals.com), Crumpler & Co. Personal Financial Counselors (http://www.crumplercompany.com), Leonard Weissbach (http://www.business-affairs.com), myCFO. com (http://www.mycfo.com), and WealthPlace.com (http:// www.wealthplace.com).

DEVELOP A HIGHLY PROFESSIONAL WEB SITE

A HIGH-NET-WORTH market strategy requires a very slick site. Expect to spend considerably more on both development and maintenance of such a site. The site needs to exude professionalism and class. It is important that the site give the visitor the feeling that you are very capable and experienced in dealing with the needs of the wealthy. You can also assume a greater bandwidth capability for most of your site's visitors. HNW individuals are used to having the best and are likely to purchase top-of-the-line systems and ISP connections, which means you can allow your Web designer greater flexibility in the use of graphics, audio, splash screens, and even video. Remember that these prospects expect the highest level of quality. (Note: This isn't a license to go graphics- and audio-crazy. Whatever you develop must be restrained and tastefully done. The keyword here is *classy*.)

Most of the site functionality and components suggested for the *customer service* site (Chapter 1) also apply to an HNW site. In addition, you need to highlight those services that differentiate you from the typical financial services firm. These services might include facilitating tax preparation, accounting, or legal services (through partnerships with CPAs or attorneys who also cater to HNW individuals). They could also include research on charitable organizations for gift-giving and wealth-transfer needs or research on assisted living options for family members. You may offer general family services such as staff employment and administration, home and automobile purchasing, travel arrangements, and so on. Whatever these services are, you need to be sure they are prominently featured, along with an explanation of how the client benefits from these services.

You should provide links to sites that truly cater to the HNW market. By bringing these sites together in one place, you provide a service to your prospects and clients, since it's time-consuming for them to weed through the pretenders to find useful sites. In addition, this feature, if done well, will encourage return traffic to your site. Also provide a place for prospects and clients to suggest new links (they are obviously the best source). As you might have guessed, this type of site requires a custom design and financial service experience, so try using AdvisorSites or a similar type of developer.

CONTRACT WITH A WEBCASTING SITE AND WEBCAST SPECIAL EVENTS

CREATE AND PROMOTE special events designed exclusively for the wealthy. These events can be online, in person, or both. The key is that they revolve around topics of interest to those with high net worth. Some firms in this niche offer an annual retreat where their clients have an opportunity to network, and the firm facilitates discussion topics.

Webcasting HNW events has some distinct advantages. First, the wealthy, particularly the very wealthy, tend to be geographically dispersed (some have multiple homes). It is difficult to find a central location for an event that they will find attractive (particularly within reasonable budget constraints). Second, these people are very jealous of their time, and it is hard to develop a compelling reason for them to give up the time to attend. Webcasting reduces both of these problems since it allows your event to reach a widely dispersed audience and makes it easier to participate because they are not required to go anywhere. You can also offer a recorded version of your event for people who were unable to attend live. See Chapter 2 for more information on Webcasting and online events.

SET UP YOUR CONTACT MANAGEMENT SYSTEM TO SEND REGULAR MARKETING AND CUSTOMER SERVICE E-MAILS

CONSTRUCT YOUR E-MAIL list as discussed in Chapter 3, "Direct E-mail Marketing." Be sure your marketing e-mails promote the unique services you offer HNW individuals. Again, you want to distinguish yourself from the crowd of financial service providers bidding to get their attention. Be sure your client service e-mails include reminders of local charitable or social occasions that your clients have expressed interest in. Your list of personal services will also offer additional chances to contact them for regularly scheduled services.

CAREFULLY PLAN YOUR E-MAIL DESIGN, CONTENT, AND TIMING

IN ADDITION TO THE methods for constructing a program of marketing e-mails discussed in Chapter 3, you need to raise the visual quality of your e-mail. Earlier I mentioned that e-mails should focus on content and not on visuals. That is only partially true for the HNW market. Here the content and visuals need to be equally compelling.

There are two ways to attack this problem. You can keep your e-mail elegant but simple with links back to your Web site for more visually stimulating content, or you can make your e-mail visually exciting by adding color and graphics. Of these two options, the former is the better choice. E-mail systems still vary too much in sophistication, and some ISPs have limitations on e-mail size. Either of these two situations could cause your graphically intense e-mail not to be received properly. By providing links back to your site, you can present your message very dramatically on an HTML Web page dedicated to that purpose (or alternatively with a PDF file that will load automatically). This approach also allows you to use your Web designer to assist in the layout of your marketing material.

Physician Marketing

YOUR TARGET IS DOCTORS. Most of your income comes from very targeted estate planning, endowments, financial planning, tax planning, and personal services to those with high net worth. Thus, your current marketing strategy is based on *expertise* and *image.*

The physician marketing strategy is really a variation of HNW marketing, but it is focused exclusively on physicians. As such, it also uses online support to more efficiently access market information, locate potential prospects, and offer more personalized service. The principal online channels used in this strategy are search engines/directories, a specialized Web site, e-mail, Webcasting services, and a contact management system. Here are the steps necessary to develop this strategy:

DO AN INTERNET SEARCH TO FIND SOME USEFUL SITES

HERE ARE SOME Web sites to start with. Do keep in mind that the more narrow the market (as in this example), the more intensive your search will be. However, many of the guidelines given for the HNW searches apply here as well. Keywords include *physician Web sites, physician financial services, physician financial advice, physician asset management, physician market, doctor financial services,* and *physician mailing lists.*

◆ **Articles on the physician market.** Some articles have been published on physician financial planning and financial services, but in general, not as much as for the larger HNW market. Two examples are "Don't Let Your Dream Retirement Turn into a Nightmare," *Physician's Practice Digest* (http://www.ppdnet.com/content/issues/janfeb99/retire.htm) and "Retirement Planning for Physicians after the Taxpayer Relief Act of 1997," Law Offices of James Lange, from the *Roth IRA Advisor* (http://www.rothira-advisor.com/physicians.htm). Baylor College of Medicine Financial Planning Forum (http://www.bcm.tmc.edu/planned_giving/) has an archive of articles on a variety of financial planning and estate planning topics.

◆ **Consultants.** Farris Group (http://www.farrisgroup.com) is a physician market research firm that provides market assessments for physicians. However, much of this information is very useful to you as well.

◆ **CPA physician specialists.** The MD Taxes Network is a CPA firm that specializes in physician services (http://www.mdtaxes.com). Partnering with firms like this can be very lucrative, and the Internet facilitates long-distance relationships that would have been unworkable only a few years ago.

◆ **Mailing lists.** Two list brokers that specialize in physician lists are Direct Mail Connection (http://www.directmailconnection.com/mailing-lists/medicalmailinglists.html) and SK&A Information Services (http://www.skainfo.com).

◆ **Publications.** I was able to locate several good books. The first is a bit long in the tooth but still excellent: *Physician Financial Planning in a Changing Environment,* by Russ Alan Prince, 1996 (http://medicalbookstore.com—look under practice management). The second is brand-new: *2001 Financial Planning for Physicians and Healthcare Professionals* by David E. Marcinko, CFP, from Harcourt Professional Publishing (http://www.hpponline.com/catalog/0-15-607028-6.shtml). I also found a print newsletter devoted to the physician's financial needs, *Physicians Financial News* (http://news.medscape.com/PFNPublishing/PhysiciansFinancialNews/public/PFN-about.html). This publication offers not only insights into the type of help physicians are looking for and some suggested solutions but also an advertising vehicle. MDOptions.com (http://mdoptions.com) is an online publication with current news affecting physicians.

◆ **Sites for physicians.** There are literally thousands of medically related sites on the Web. Many of these offer the occasion to do research on your market, provide advertising opportunities, or simply offer links useful to physician clients that you can add to your Web site. Just a few examples: HCPro.com (http://www.hcpro.com) for physician regulatory and compliance info; Student Doctor Network (http://studentdoctor.net), a network of physicians in training that includes chat rooms and bulletin boards; Medscape (http://www.medscape.com), the largest and most visited physician site; Physician's Online Network (http://www.po.com), which facilitates physician networking—though this does require a physician registration, one of your clients may be willing to assist you here; and Physician Marketing Consultants (http://marketingfor docs.com), which provides consulting advice to physicians on how to market their practices.

◆ **Web developers.** Just as there are specialist developers in the financial services arena, so there are some specialist developers for physician practices. Providing a lead or link to such a vendor can be a value-added service to offer the physician. Two such developers are CopelyNet Physician Web sites (http://home.epix.net/~djcopely/main.html) and Medplaza, Inc. (http://www.med plaza.com/med).

◆ **Competitors.** As always, looking at your competitors (large and small) is revealing. Here are a few: American Physician Service Group, Inc. (http://www.amph.com), Jarvis and Mandell LLC (http://www.jarvisandmandell.com), and Physician Asset Management, Inc. (http://www.physassetmgmt.com).

The remaining steps in physician marketing are as explained earlier in the HNW strategy.

PART

TWO

ADVANCED CYBER-MARKETING

HERE IS YOUR reference guide to Web marketing. As with any reference manual, take some time and browse the topic headings. Look for subjects that fit with your marketing strategy and market niche. If you started with a strategy developed in the earlier chapters or if you are currently working a niche not previously discussed, use this reference area to fill out your thinking. There are also a number of marketing approaches presented here that you can use to supplement an existing strategy.

Remember, too, that time has a way of changing priorities and filling in experience. What seems too technical today may be just what you need in six months. A marketing approach that appears far afield may be exactly the approach you're looking for next year. So revisit this section from time to time.

CHAPTER

5

REACH OUT AND TOUCH SOMEONE

Prospecting Online

ONCE YOU DETERMINE your target audience, you need to figure out how to reach them online. As a caution, remember that the demographics of the Internet are different from those of the population at large. Don't assume that you know what that demographic is. For example, one of the fastest-growing groups of Internet users is people over age sixty-five—a group that at first blush would appear to be less likely to adopt new technology. Some good sites to do your initial research include:

◆ **The U.S. Census** (http://www.census.gov). There is a wealth of very specific demographic information in this huge site. Particularly useful is the "American Fact Finder." This is extremely easy to use and allows you to break down characteristics like type of employment, education, income, and so on, all the way down to city or county. This becomes increasingly important in both e-mail and Web-based marketing since your prospect could be from anywhere you are licensed.

◆ **The CommerceNet Research Center** (http://www.commerce .net/research/). This site takes the heartbeat of the Internet, so to speak. The most recent national surveys of Internet use are available here, including e-commerce and demographic breakdowns. You can also access Gideon (Gateway to Internet Demographics Online) from here. This is a fee-based service that will break down Internet use by age, gender, education, race, occupation, PC ownership, credit card ownership, primary location, children, income, and more.

◆ **MarketResearch.com** (http://www.marketresearch.com) is an extraordinarily rich site with thousands of research reports that profile a wide range of possible target markets. This is also a fee-based service, though many of the free summaries or abstracts contain a level of detail that is useful in reviewing an unfamiliar market. Use the "find" search function to quickly get the information you need.

◆ **The Yahoo! Marketing and Advertising section** contains links to a number of online Internet research services (http://dir. yahoo.com/Business_and_Economy/Companies/Marketing_and _Advertising/Internet/Market_Research/). This will help you begin to profile the type of potential prospects using online services. Many of these focus on different market segments.

What follows is a discussion on how you can use online technology to better prospect for new customers. There are two types of prospecting that most professionals use currently. There is *active prospecting,* in which you are proactively going after new prospects, and *passive prospecting,* when you are encouraging the potential prospect to contact you. The chart at right lists the various methods discussed in this section.

Active Prospecting—"Hello, My Name Is ..."

ACTIVE PROSPECTING MEANS you take the initiative to reach prospects directly. Unless you've been living on an undiscovered tropical island in the central Pacific and the term "computer" is

Active Prospecting Techniques

1 E-mail Marketing
   a. E-mail Lists and List Brokers
   b. List Management and List Management Firms
   c. Legal and Ethical List Management and
      Spamming Issues
2 Online Sales Seminars
3 Online Sales Presentations
4 Traditional Active Marketing Goes Online

Passive Prospecting Techniques

1 Internet Advertising
2 E-mail Newsletters and E-zines
3 Listing with Search Services
4 Listing in Specialized Directories
   a. Yellow Page Listings
   b. Business Directories
5 Online Referral Services
6 Online Classified Ads
7 Online Informational Seminars
8 Web Site Sponsorship
9 Writing for Web Sites
10 Traditional Passive Marketing Goes Online

new to you, the "@" symbol signifying an e-mail address has become all-too familiar. If you want to reach Bob Smith via e-mail, you simply type in Bob's e-mail address, such as bsmith@isp.com. That's simple enough.

Hold on! It's not quite *that* simple! Unlike a street address or a phone number, an e-mail address *changes* when you change Internet providers or e-mail hosting services (imagine if you had to use a different street address for your clients depending on whether you use the post office or Federal Express). Since e-mail address changes can happen frequently as people become disenchanted with a particular provider or upgrade to a hot new service, keeping an accurate e-mail address list is like hitting a moving target.

That's bad enough, but it's only part of the story. Increasingly, people have multiple e-mail addresses (sometimes with different providers). They may use one at work, one for general correspondence, and another for friends. Plus, each member of the family may have an individual e-mail address.

So where do you go to get accurate e-mail address information, and how do you use those addresses to market your products and services? What follows are some of the methods and players involved in e-mail marketing.

E-MAIL LISTS AND LIST BROKERS

SOME FIRMS WILL SELL their company list of names and e-mail addresses. Many traditional list brokers now offer e-mail lists. However, these lists are created in a very different manner from traditional lists. One option is for the firm to create an opt-in/opt-out Web page, which allows subscribers to "option in" or "option out" on a special Web page attached to a database. Users maintain control of their status.

The opt-in/opt-out Web page is designed to allow each subscriber to answer a series of questions (usually in exchange for some product or service of value to the subscriber). For example, these questions may gather information on age, level of education, household income, occupation, or product and service interests. They may also capture prospect and customer likes and dislikes as well as demographics and lifestyle.

Another option is for the list broker to purchase a list from another company that has received authorization from the consumers to sell their list of names. Examples might include a business's customer list, a newsletter subscriber list, a chat room participant list, etc. The list usually comes with a number of restrictions on its use by the list owner or the customer.

Finally, the list could be proprietary. That is, it was created by another division of that list broker as part of the services it offers to the consumer (this could be almost anything from magazine publishing to chat rooms). The customers have given the company permission to sell their e-mail addresses. This is usually in exchange for free or discounted products or services.

Some list brokers specialize in e-mail marketing. Examples of such list brokers are TargetPacks.com (http://www.targetpacks.com), PostMasterDirect.com (http://www.postmasterdirect.com), BulletMail (http://www.bulletmail.com), Liszt (http://www.liszt.com), yesmail.com (http://www.yesmail.com), Netcreations (http://www.netcreations.com), 24/7 Media (http://www.247media.com), and MatchLogic (http://www.matchlogic.com/index.asp).

The simplest way to use these lists is to purchase one from a list broker. The cost is based on the selectivity of the list and the number of names you purchase. Charges vary widely from vendor to vendor, so check around. The biggest limitation of purchased lists is that geographically limited lists are difficult to find—thus you may be purchasing leads that are outside your license area. However, larger offices or offices that partner up for marketing purposes can make this approach workable.

Even if you can find lists that are targeted for the correct geographic area, they may not be the correct demographic. Remember that the tenets from "Prospecting 101" still apply to e-mail lists. A list with a larger number of names does not mean a list with more prospects. It is better to pay more for a list that has been culled of those individuals who don't meet your market profile. For example, if you are promoting estate planning, a list of predominantly young people is not efficient. Also, be sure that your list has been validated recently. E-mail addresses change much more frequently than phone numbers or street addresses (your list broker should provide you with this information).

Caution: Any e-mail lists purchased like this should include only "opt-in" or proprietary lists for which the list broker has been given permission by those named on the list to use their e-mail address in a direct marketing effort like yours—otherwise, sending e-mails to these individuals constitutes spamming (see "Legal and Ethical List Management and Spamming Issues" later in this chapter).

It is common to find no single source with a good e-mail list for your area and market. Don't give up. It takes a bit longer, but you can build your prospect list from a number of different sources. In fact, it is a good practice to maintain your own database of opt-in e-mail prospects. That way you can continually add new names as you come across them. Sources include list brokers, referrals, opt-in visitors to your Web site, and your existing database of prospects. Yahoo! Groups can help you with this effort (www.groups.yahoo.com). This site will let you create your own mailing list online and send regular e-newsletters for free. Spark-LIST.com offers a bit more robust fee-based service (http://www.sparklist.com).

You can even do an online lookup of e-mail addresses for your current database of prospect names using names and addresses. There are a number of specialized search engines for finding e-mail addresses. Some examples include: The Internet @ddress Finder (http://www.iaf.net), Yahoo! People Search (http://people.yahoo.com), WhoWhere? People Finder (http://www.who where.lycos.com), and Bigfoot (http://www.bigfoot.com).

LIST MANAGEMENT AND LIST MANAGEMENT FIRMS

ONCE YOU HAVE THE LIST, you need to manage it. E-mail lists are much more complex to maintain than traditional lists. People change Internet providers frequently, which causes e-mail addresses to changes frequently as well. In many cases, you have no way to know about a change unless you have an electronic monitor in place.

Depending on the size of the list and the complexity of your marketing efforts, you may want to do it yourself or investigate an e-mail list management service. Sometimes the list broker offers these services. If not, some firms specialize in this kind of support. Two of the largest are Messagemedia (http://www.message media.com) and DoubleClick (http://www.doubleclick.net/us/), both of which offers a complete line of list management services and software. More typical of the smaller firms is Hutchins & Associates (http://www.wwwdotcom.com/mailinglist.html).

If you have a small office, an alternative is to purchase list management software. Two examples are ListMate (http://www.global-ventures.com/listmate/) and Satori Software's Bulk Mailer (http://www.satorisw.com). Still another solution is to purchase software that will translate e-mail address information or lists for your contact management system. One such vendor is eGrabber (http://www.egrabber.com). These approaches can be less costly, but they also provide less support.

Another simple solution for the small office is to employ a free reminder service like LifeMinders.com (http://www.life minders.com). LifeMinders.com will automatically send out, to any number of people, reminders for birthdays, anniversaries, or other events. Once you register, you get a notice whenever the message should be sent.

Most list management services and some software allow you to build your own opt-in/opt-out database on your computer or Web site (depending on access). This allows you more flexibility, since you can not only add new prospects to the database at will but also drop in purchased lists from list brokers. Some of these management services also allow you to store your database on their server, where it is maintained by experienced professionals using systems designed specifically to protect list integrity and security. For example, they can handle opt-out requests and undeliverable e-mail quickly and easily.

Also, most list management services or software will allow you to create and manage your own campaign. You can configure e-mail marketing campaigns to segments of your list or to an entire database. You can personalize and customize messages and deliver them in a variety of e-mail formats. Then the system will broadcast all of your e-mails quickly and efficiently to your entire list or to specific subsets. You can send newsletters, coupons, invoices/statements, announcements, and more. You can even conduct surveys to gather in-depth information. Many also offer auto-responder technology to allow immediate response to questions, comments, concerns, or orders.

Many list management services and some software will also measure the success of your campaign by tracking responses and giving you reports, plus monitoring your list and the status of your mailings.

LEGAL AND ETHICAL LIST MANAGEMENT AND SPAMMING ISSUES

THERE ARE NO SPECIFIC LAWS governing spamming (although there are several pending federal bills), but the Internet has developed some increasingly effective tools that can and will be used against spammers. Note: It doesn't take a mass mailing to trigger an accusation of spamming. It only takes a few disgruntled recipients who file complaints. A number of watchdog sites take complaints about spammers. Typical is CAUCE (Coalition Against Unsolicited Commercial E-mail) (http://www.cauce.org). Links from this site should give you some idea of what the response can be. Some examples include being submitted and labeled as a spammer on screening software, being posted as a blacklist spammer and thus having major list brokers refuse to do business with you, or having a lawsuit filed against you for invasion of privacy. Although CAUCE is not officially sanctioned by any regulatory bodies, this issue is still in its infancy, and this group has the largest following.

What exactly is spam? CAUCE and other organizations define it in two general ways: (1) unwanted or unsolicited e-mail messages or mailing-list or newsgroup postings, and (2) advertisements or solicitations to large numbers of unsolicited recipients, usually via mailing lists or newsgroups.

Remember that feelings on this issue can run high. The following guidelines are offered as a statement of Internet standards and best current practices for proper mailing-list management. Follow these steps (or make sure your list manager follows them) and you will keep yourself out of trouble. In addition, many compliance departments have developed specific guidelines on spamming—so be sure you check.

◆ The e-mail addresses of new subscribers must be confirmed or verified before mailings commence. The originator of the e-mail sends a message to potential subscribers, and they reply back to complete the subscription. However, there are numerous ways to confirm or verify an e-mail address in order to ensure that mailing lists are not used for abusive purposes, such as search engines that specialize in finding e-mail addresses.

◆ You or the mailing list administrator should always include at the beginning of your e-mail message your name, physical address, and phone number.

◆ You or the mailing list administrator must provide a simple method for subscribers to terminate their subscriptions and clear and effective instructions for unsubscribing from a mailing list. Mailings from a list must cease promptly once a subscription is terminated.

◆ You or the mailing list administrator should provide an e-mail address to which messages may be sent for further contact via e-mail or telephone. This is for those who wish to terminate their mailing list subscriptions but are unable or unwilling to follow standard automated procedures.

◆ Invalid or undeliverable addresses must be pruned, or you must take steps to ensure that mailings do not overwhelm less robust hosts or networks.

◆ The mailing list administrator or you should maintain a "suppression list" of e-mail addresses from which all subscription requests are rejected.

◆ You or the mailing list administrator must make adequate disclosures about how subscriber addresses will be used, including whether or not addresses are subject to sale or trade with other parties. These disclosures must be included at the end of every e-mail, or the e-mail must include a link back to a site.

◆ Once a mailing list is traded or sold, it may no longer be an opt-in mailing list. Therefore, those who are acquiring opt-in lists from others must examine the terms and conditions under which the addresses were originally compiled and determine that all recipients have, in fact, opted in specifically to the mailing lists to which they are being traded or sold.

◆ Adequate disclosures must be made about the nature of your mailing lists, including the subject matter of the lists and anticipated frequency of messages. A substantive change in either the subject matter or frequency of messages may constitute a new and separate mailing list, requiring a separate subscription.

◆ You or the mailing list administrator should create a new mailing list when there is a substantive change in either the subject matter or frequency of messages.

ONLINE SALES SEMINARS

IF YOU ARE CURRENTLY USING a sales seminar model for marketing, why not move your seminar online? It is now possible to hold a simultaneous virtual meeting with individuals from widely different geographic locations.

An online seminar (Webcast, Web conference, or virtual conference) is the combination of a phone call or Internet call with live Web-based visuals and interaction. For example, you can load a PowerPoint seminar presentation from your computer to the server hosting the online seminar (local or remote) and then give the audience the URL. Participants who log on can share in the visual presentation and interact with each other from the comfort of their office, home, or wherever they may be at the time.

These virtual seminars have a number of advantages over their physical counterparts. First, participants find it much easier to attend (they merely log on instead of getting a babysitter, driving to a location, finding a parking place, and then driving home when it is over). Second, the ease of attendance can increase the number of participants. Third, it is not necessary to find a central location to hold the seminar. Fourth, the cost of renting facilities and equipment, duplicating presentation materials, and providing refreshments is reduced or eliminated. Of course, before giving any online presentations, you will need to get your seminar or conference script reviewed by your compliance department.

You can literally present any type of audio or visual content that you can present in person while interacting with your audience and receiving real-time feedback. Presentation possibilities include PowerPoint slides, annotation tools, live software demonstrations, polling, white boards, Web tours, and streaming audio and video. You can also control the level and ways your audience interacts with you, including participants' ability to type in or ask questions, review slides, and chat with each other.

It is not all roses, however. Some technical hurdles and costs must be borne to do a seminar this way. You need specialized software (you can purchase and install this yourself, but unless you specialize in seminars of this type, you might want to rent the services you need). The other problem is an uneven distribution of online technology among your prospects. Most software available now considers these limitations and allows you to adjust your presentation to the receiving technology. Finally, you need to be sure your site clearly indicates where you are licensed to do business.

Many of the software vendors that specialize in sales of this type of software offer virtual Webcast hosting as well. There is even a new entity called an Application Service Provider (ASP) that specializes in online seminars, offering several brands of conferencing software and many other services up to and including full meeting facilitation. Given the wide range in cost, available services, and quality among these vendors, you will need to match the type of vendor you select to the meeting size and frequency, the complexity of your presentation, and the sophistication of the audience.

The range in cost (at the time we went to press) for hosted presentation services begins at $10 per user or use (plus a $50 setup fee) for Active Touches' WebEx (http://www.webex.com), all the way up to PlaceWare at $400 per seat for an annual unlimited use agreement (http://placeware.com). The cost to purchase the software also varies widely. The following vendors sell software or host presentations:

◆ **Astound** (http://www.astound.com). Sales and hosting.

◆ **Cisco Systems' Cisco Seminars and Events Online** (http:// webevents.broadcast.com/cisco/ciscolive/home.asp). Sales only—high-end system for large meetings.

◆ **Epiphany's iMeet** (http://imeet.com). Hosting only—free use for fewer than five users and less than sixty minutes—a simple system best for small meetings.

◆ **Evoke Communications** (http://www.evoke.com). Sales and hosting—sophisticated system, excellent for large seminars.

◆ **Microsoft's NetMeeting** (http://www.microsoft.com/win dows/netmeeting/?RLD=52). Sales only—simple system, best for small meetings.

◆ **PlaceWare** (http://www.placeware.com). Sales—sophisticated system, excellent for large seminars. ASP hosting—platform is available at a lower one-time-event cost. Full meeting support and services available, including marketing, reminders, billing, etc.

◆ **Seminar Source.com** (http://www.seminarsource.com). ASP hosting only. Platform is available at a lower one-time-event cost. Full meeting support and services available, including reminders, billing, marketing, etc.

◆ **WebEx.com** (http://www.webex.com). ASP hosting only. Platform is available at a lower one-time-event cost. Full meeting support and services available.

ONLINE SALES PRESENTATIONS

ALTHOUGH ONE-ON-ONE online videophone presentations are not yet practical for use with the public, it is very possible to develop an online presentation that you can view simultaneously with a client or prospect while interacting over the phone or via computer.

This type of presentation is most useful for potential customers who are remote from your office. This approach does not require much Internet savvy, just your marketing skill and some time spent learning how to construct an online presentation.

If you want to develop your own online presentations, visit Presenters Online (http://presentersonline.com). This site contains a wealth of information specifically designed for presenters. It includes presentation training (including how to develop a presentation in PowerPoint and convert it for use online), resources like templates and clip art, and a great help section (with real people to answer your questions). You can even join their Presenter Club and network with other presenters.

Some of the vendors that specialize in smaller online conferences (mentioned earlier for seminar Webcasting support) are good choices for working with individual clients. Most have lower pricing for small events (fewer than five attendees)—in some cases, it is even free.

Assuming your prospect has a printer, you can take this approach a few steps further. You can usually obtain online versions of most of the forms your prospect needs to complete the transaction from your broker-dealer. These can then be e-mailed to your prospect at the end of your presentation and completed while you have the person on the phone.

TRADITIONAL ACTIVE MARKETING GOES ONLINE

EVEN MORE TRADITIONAL marketing approaches can be made more efficient by going online to find the support you need. For example, doing targeted direct mailings or telemarketing is easier with the Internet. You supply the criteria, and myprospects.com (http://myprospects.com), Seisint (http://www.seisint.com), Find-MoreBuyers.com (http://www.findmorebuyers.com), or zap-data.com (http://zapdata.com) can generate prospect mail or phone lists based on those parameters. Then use eGrabber (http://www.egrabber.com) to translate the addresses into your contact management system.

In addition, FindMoreBuyers.com and PerformanceData (http://www.performancedata.com) also offer a database marketing approach. Once you provide various types of demographic information about your clients, they can generate a list of potential clients that match those profiles.

Even more-traditional list brokers are offering online services to assist in selecting the right mailing lists for your target market. Some examples are Judy Diamond Associates (http://www.judy diamond.com/index.html) and the American List Counsel (http://www.amlist.com). Thomson Financial Wealth Identification (http://www.wealthid.com) offers a series of online tools that can help you locate wealthy individuals or those high-net-worth employees of public companies with executive stock option programs. Who$Wealthy.com (http://www.whoswealthy.net) offers lists of wealthy prospects online. USADATA (http://usadata.com) has completely automated the print mailing process. You log on to their site, select from preapproved sales materials provided by your broker-dealer, determine the geography and type of prospect you want to mail, add your address info, and they print, stuff and mail it for you! (Note: Your broker-dealer needs to have an agreement with the USADATA for the process to be fully automated.)

To save you time, here is a meta search engine site already configured to do a search across most major search engines looking for list brokers (http://pluto.metagopher.com/nph-gopher .go?w=list%20broker&m=100175). Enter this URL and you will get a list of links to most major list broker sites.

Passive Prospecting—
"Stop By and Let's Talk ..."

PASSIVE PROSPECTING MEANS that you indirectly encourage your prospect to come to you. There are many forms and degrees of passive prospecting, including banner ads or links on other sites, advertisements on voluntary e-mail list groups or e-zines, listings in search engines or directories, online informational seminars, sponsoring topical Web sites, and of course, functions within your own Web site. These can range from simply listing your business name and contact information to complex marketing efforts. The common thread is that all require the user to take some action that requests a response from you.

A caution: Passive advertising should only supplement, not replace, other forms of active marketing. All passive advertising is inherently limited because it requires you to wait for the prospect to act: The prospects must find your ad or listing before they can do anything.

The Internet is unlike any other medium due to the layers of complexity it employs. For example, a search engine is more like a card in the library's card catalog than it is a phone directory. Just because a book is listed in a card catalog doesn't mean anyone knows it's there, much less has read it. Now, let's look at some of the many passive ad or listing options available.

INTERNET ADVERTISING

◆ **What is it?** Businesses use one of two basic models to operate in cyberspace. The first is the online storefront model. This is a company that has moved all or a portion of its business online. Here the primary source of revenue to the site owner is direct sales of products and services through the site. However, in many cases, additional revenue to the site owner is generated from advertising by third parties. Examples of this model are abundant and include:

Individual retail merchant sites like 1-800-Flowers (http://www.1800flowers.com/) or Amazon.com (http://www.amazon.com)

Online shopping malls like CitiMall.com (http://www.
citimall.com)

Manufacturers' direct sales sites like Dell Computers (http://
www.dell.com/us/en/gen/default.htm)

The second basic model is the sponsored site, in which the
primary source of revenue to the site owner is site advertisers.
Currently, there are three major categories of advertiser-
supported sites:

Sponsored content sites like Hotwired (http://hotwired.lycos.
com), ESPN (http://espn.go.com), and ZDNet (http://
www.zdnet.com)

Sponsored search agents and directories like Go.com (http://
infoseek.go.com), Excite (http://www.excite.com), and Yahoo!
(http://www.yahoo.com)

Entry portal sites like Netscape (http://home.netscape.com)[1]

The most common form of advertising on either model is the
banner ad. Banner ads are simply ads you purchase on other Web
sites. They are small, typically rectangular, graphic images that are
linked to a *target ad.* Banner ads provide little information. In some
cases, they exclude even the identity of the advertiser. They serve as
an invitation for the visitor to click on the banner to learn more.
Some incorporate motion or sound as an additional enticement.
Target ads, on the other hand, can be very involved, ranging from
a single Web page with basic HTML to a complete Web site. These
ads are triggered either by a banner ad or "pop-up" when you enter
a site or page.

An alternative to the banner ad or target ad is to request a link
to your Web site on another site. This approach presupposes that
your site's content offers something of value to the visitors to the
site to which you want to link.

◆ **How do I use it?** You have many choices when it comes to Internet advertising. A number of firms specialize in Internet advertising
placement. They offer a number of ways to pay for their services,
which can become very confusing. Fortunately, there are several
excellent reference sites covering most of the available options and
linking to the firms that can place the ads. The first is Adbility.com
(http://www.adbility.com). It is a great general resource and even

helps you avoid vendors using questionable practices. Some other excellent sources are Webref's section on Web site promotion (http://webreference.com/promotion/index.html), Ad Resource (http://adres.internet.com), and AdCentral (http://www.adcentral.com). If you would rather "cut to the chase," you can contact the ad placement service directly. An excellent service is DoubleClick (http://www.doubleclick.net), which not only places the ads for you but also provides assistance in ad layout and design. (Caution: While this is an excellent ad placement vehicle, avoid using their preference-tracking capabilities, due to privacy concerns. This company has been charged by Internet watchdog groups with engaging in unfair and deceptive trade practices by tracking the online activities of Internet users and combining that tracking data with detailed, personal information on identifiable individuals contained in a massive national marketing database. This litigation is still pending.)

Internet advertising is usually purchased on a "cost per thousand impressions" basis, or CPM. An impression ("exposure" or "page view") means that a visitor views a target ad page or site. In other words, whenever a page is "served" to your computer screen, measurement software counts the "impression."

Ads can be placed anywhere on a page, although ads are more successful when they are displayed in the top half of the page ("above the fold"). This placement will deliver higher click-throughs than the same ad placed at the bottom of a page.[2] Ads next to the right scroll bar generate a 228 percent higher click-through rate than ads at the top margin of the page.[3]

A common banner ad package consists of 100,000 impressions, costing anywhere from $5 to $100 per thousand ($25 to $70 CPM is average for popular sites). Keep in mind that most sites have repeat visitors, and most visitors view more than a single page of information, so your 100,000 impressions could actually represent only about 10,000 to 40,000 unique visitors.

Be sure you read the fine print. In some cases, the number of impressions is guaranteed, while in others, it is estimated. Some sites charge a flat rate for estimated impressions, then charge for "overdeliveries." Other sites do not impose an extra charge for overdeliveries. Most popular sites offer ad agency discounts and volume or frequency discounts. The ad agency rate, known as the net rate, is typically a 15 percent discount from the gross rate. You may be able to get this discount if you agree to a certain contract level and you do the ad without agency involvement.

Avoid any ad arrangement that asks you to pay for the number of "hits" on your ad. "Hits" and "page hits" (in contrast to impressions) are registered every time any text or graphic file is delivered, *whether advertising is displayed or not.* A page hit, or HTML hit, is registered every time a complete HTML page, including text and graphic files, is delivered (again, whether advertising is displayed or not). The ratio can easily be two to four page hits to actual impressions.[4]

As you can tell, this approach to advertising places a premium on site traffic. The more traffic a site has, the greater your chances of a potential prospect from your geographic area locating your ad. To find out which sites had the most traffic last month, check out the latest free rankings at Media Metrix (http://www.mediametrix.com) or the top 100 by category at Go2Net Network's 100Hot (http://www.100hot.com/index.html). You can cross-check those listings through PC Data Online Reports. You can also get more extensive listings of the top 2,500 sites, although there is a significant fee.

A low-cost alternative is to join a banner exchange. The largest is Microsoft BCentral Banner Network (http://adnetwork.bcentral.com). This network is an association of more than 400,000 Web sites that trade banner advertising space with one another—for free. For every two ads you show on your site, you earn one credit to have your banner shown on another member's site. A more targeted site is the Financial Ad Trader, which specializes in financially oriented sites (http://www.adtrader.com). The vast majority of these sites have very low traffic, but you can't beat the price!

Of course, if you discover a particular Web site that you think might be a good fit for your geographic area and type of prospect, you can always approach the company directly. A good way to attack this is to search for local businesses or malls that have Web sites. Simply do a search using the business name and then check the address on the site to be sure it is the same business. Alternatively, search on the name of a community (if it is a common name, include the state name or abbreviation as well). You will also find some local online malls, such as the SavannaNow Online Mall (http://www.marketplacenow.com/mall/index.html).

Most sizable communities also have one or more community sites or portals. For example, Omaha, Nebraska, has Omaha.com (http://omaha.com) and DiscoverOmaha.com (http://www.discoveromaha.com).

Since these types of sites focus on serving the local area, the chances are greater that their advertisers are also local. Still another approach is to start with online yellow pages directories. Many of these also list the company's Web site. Keep in mind that some local nonprofits also have Web sites that allow advertising or site sponsorship. Taking a community approach has an additional advantage: Most of these sites have much lower traffic than the larger regional or national sites and thus are more reasonably priced.

There are a number of ways to get other sites linked to your Web site. The most obvious is to approach the site directly by sending an e-mail indicating your interest in a link. Start by focusing on sites that cover topics that would be of interest to your target audience (use a search engine or directory to assist you). Sites cater to the needs of such diverse groups as business owners, people age fifty and older, gardeners, investment clubs, etc. Be prepared for the fact that some sites will not accept links. However, many more do allow such links. Since your site is likely to have a relatively low volume of traffic, you will probably have to pay for the link. The cost varies widely, but the higher the traffic to a site, the more it will cost. Be leery of sites that offer free links, because you usually get what you pay for. Some commercial sites have a link exchange program, and thus the link can be free as long as you allow a link to their site from yours.

ADVERTISE IN E-MAIL NEWSLETTERS OR E-ZINES
◆ **What are they?** Computers linked to the Internet have introduced electronic newsletters, e-mail newsletters, and e-zines (electronic magazines). An e-zine (pronounced "e-zeen") regularly

sends articles, news, and other useful information on a given topic to an e-mail list. E-zines come in a variety of electronic formats but are most often distributed via e-mail or the Web. Web-based e-zines are sometimes called Web-zines. The major difference is that Web-zines have the majority of their content posted on Web sites, with links embedded in the text of a distributed e-mail.

◆ **How do I use them?** There are literally thousands of e-zines being published on the Web every day. Unfortunately, about 90 percent of these are very poorly done (with readers you don't want as clients) or they have very limited circulation (the five people who read this e-zine might become clients, but they are hardly worth the effort). Compounding this difficulty is that many e-zines do not accept advertising. So how do you cut through the maze and get at the publications you want to reach?

The first step is to get a feel for the types of newsletters available. One place to start is Ezine-Universe.com (http://Ezine-Universe.com)—a searchable directory of more than 1,600 e-mail-delivered e-zines—you can narrow down the newsletters that your potential prospects might be reading. Then check out http://BestEzines.com/ for reviews of the best e-zines in more than twenty categories.

You then can either approach the individual publication directly (cheaper, but time-consuming) or contract advertising through an aggregator like List-Universe (http://www.list-universe.com), which provides ad placement services to reach targeted audiences via contracted opt-in e-mail newsletters and opt-in discussion lists.

ADVERTISE BY LISTING WITH SEARCH SERVICES

◆ **What are search engines?** Search engines, like HotBot (http://www.HotBot.com), create their listings automatically. Search engines "crawl the Web," and then people search through what they have found. If you change your Web pages, search engines eventually find these changes, and that can affect how you are listed. Page titles, body copy, and other elements all play a role. This is both good and bad. On the one hand, you know that you can search according to the latest information contained on the site. What you don't know is whether some change has inadvertently removed a keyword you used in the past. On the plus side, search engines return by far the most listings. On the minus side, you are likely to get a large number of irrelevant listings since automated searches are not very intelligent.

Search engines have three major elements. First is the *spider,* also called the *crawler* or *bot.* The spider visits a Web page, reads it, and then follows links to other pages within the site. This is what it means when someone refers to a site being *spidered* or *crawled.* The spider returns to the site on a regular basis, such as every month or two, to look for changes.

Everything the spider finds goes into the second part of a search engine, the *index.* The index, sometimes called the *catalog,* is like a giant book containing a copy of every Web page the spider finds. If a Web page changes, then this book is updated with new information. Sometimes it can take a while for new pages or changes that the spider finds to be added to the index. In fact, a recent study showed that indexing of new or modified pages by just one of the major search engines can take months.[5] This can be a major drawback if your site's marketing focus changes frequently.

Search engine software is the third part of a search engine. This is the program that sifts through the millions of pages recorded in the index to find matches to a search and rank them in order of what it believes is most relevant. The ranking process is where search engines have the most trouble and where unexpected results can creep in. It is also why there are such a wide variety of results from the same inquiry made to different search engines.

Hybrid search engines also maintain an associated directory. Being included in a search engine's directory is usually a combination of luck and quality. Sometimes you can "submit" your site for review, but there is no guarantee that it will be included. Reviewers often keep an eye on sites submitted to announcement places, then choose to add those that look appealing. An example of this type of search engine is Go.com (http://www.info seek.com).

GETTING LISTED WITH A SEARCH ENGINE OR DIRECTORY

◆ **What are directories?** Many people confuse a directory (sometimes called an index) such as Yahoo! (http://www.yahoo.com) with a search engine. However, a directory doesn't use a spider; it depends on humans for its listings. Site owners submit a short description to the directory for the entire site, or editors write descriptions for sites they review. A search looks for matches only in the descriptions submitted.

Thus, changing your Web pages has no effect on your listing. Things that are useful for improving a listing with a search engine have nothing to do with improving a listing in a directory. The only exception is that a good site, with good content, might be more likely to get reviewed than a poor site.

Directories are very good at finding your target information correctly the first time. They are also good at searching when you don't have a clear idea of the keywords to use in a search. Most directories are organized with a very logical structure, which makes it easier for the user to locate information simply by browsing through the directory. However, they are far less comprehensive, and searches return a much smaller number of sites.

◆ **How do I use search services?** Well, first you have to have something for the search engine or directory to find. Unless you have a well-developed and interesting Web site, having either a search engine or directory listing is rather pointless. (See Chapter 6, "What Makes a Good Site Good?")

◆ **Which is the best?** The first question most people ask is which search engine or directory is best. There is no objective way to answer this question. Search engines and directories were created to cater to different needs, and all have a slightly different way to attack the search problem.

See Appendix B for a listing and a brief description of the major search services. Not all of the services listed in the appendix are "true" search engines that crawl the Web. For instance, Yahoo! and the Open Directory are both directories. In fact, most of the services in Appendix B are to some degree hybrids that offer both search engine and directory information, though they will feature one type of results over the other. Some services even work with other services to provide supplemental or complementary search capabilities.

One way to evaluate the different options is to go to some of the sites that have done comparisons. A good place to start is Search Engine Watch (http://searchenginewatch.com). This huge site provides a wealth of background information on search engines, how they work, search tips, site submission tips, and much more. The specific section of the site that deals with search engine comparisons is found at http://searchengine watch.com/reports/index.html. Here you will find links to all the major ratings, reviews, and tests done on search engine and directory performance.

◆ **How do I get listed?** The next most common question is how to submit a Web site URL to a search engine or directory. If you already have a site, check to see if your URL is already listed with a search engine or a directory (remember that search engines automatically look for new listings, and they may have found you). Again, Search Engine Watch is your source for a special "Check Your URL" section (http://searchenginewatch.com/webmasters/checkurl.html).

Several free services will submit your site to popular search engines and directories for you. The largest is SelfPromotion.com (http://www.selfpromotion.com). This refreshingly candid site is filled with lots of useful information and will automatically submit your site to all the major search engines and about 100 directories. NetAnnounce (http://www.netannounce.com/free.html) and Microsoft BCentral's Submit It! (http://www.submit-it.com/system/siredir.cfm?refid=49) are fee services that also offer free submission to a limited number of search services (their fee services are similar to those of Broadcaster, described below). However, all of these services are more limited in the number of search services to which they can submit, and few update your listings.

The fee services offer the advantages of less work for you, submitting your site to more search services (200 to 400 is the usual range) and regular updates. Keep in mind, though, that the size of the search engines and directories drop off quickly after the first fifty. Thus, measure the service by how comprehensive its tracking is and how often it updates your listings—not on how many search services it submits a listing to. The fee ranges from $50 to $200 per submission. An example is the British site Broadcaster (http://www.broadcaster.co.uk/). It currently submits your URL and information to more than 200 search engines and other Web media, all by your filling out a few details and hitting the broadcast button. Then you receive an e-mail response automatically telling you where and to which category your information was success-fully sent.

Submit It! is also designed to allow companies and individuals to easily, quickly, and accurately submit, track, report, and update their Web site listings to an extensive list of catalogs that have been reviewed and categorized by Submit It! researchers. They have just recently introduced regional targeting to get your listing into spe-cific regional directories.

You always have the option of doing the URL submission your-self. However, although registering a listing with a pure search engine's index would be desirable, the simple reality is that you can't. In many cases you can submit a listing to a search engine, but the real impact on a search engine listing is controlled by what you do with and to your Web site (along with factors like site traf-fic, keywords, layout, structure of the site, etc). Remember, too, that changes to your site may not affect a search engine's listings for months. (See the section on "Getting a Good Search Engine Listing," in Chapter 8.)

Directory listings are usually free, though a few offer premium positions if you pay a fee. Most directories, such as Yahoo! and Alta Vista, provide an online form on which you can submit your Web site address (URL) to be included in their index. The process for suggesting a directory listing varies somewhat from directory to directory. Yahoo!'s method can serve as an example (http://docs.yahoo.com/info/suggest/). First, you must check to see if your site is already listed. If not, you are asked to surf through the Yahoo! category listings until you find an appropriate category, at which point you click on a button on that page to suggest a site. You then complete an online form to provide a brief description, which is critical since it is the basis for any searches.

There is no guarantee that your site will be listed in the directory according to your suggestion. It is evaluated by Yahoo! to see if it fits with its organizational concept. No time frame is given for adding new sites, but expect it to take some weeks before your site appears.

◆ **How do I improve my listing?** The third most common question is how to get a listing to appear more frequently when someone does a search. You have two choices: You can either do it yourself, or you can hire a firm to do it for you. If you plan to hire some help, a couple of the better firms are listed below.

Top Site Indexing (http://www.topindex.com/services.html) offers four solutions to getting your Web site listed more frequently on the major indexes. The biggest advantage it offers is a proprietary technique to move sites up in the index listings. This service is designed for businesses that want the best value in the least time. With fees ranging from $150 to $500, it is moderately priced compared with similar services.

Calafia Consulting (http://calafia.com/services/searchengines. htm) is a more in-depth approach–a specialized consulting firm to assist you in redesigning your site to improve its listing. Calafia Consulting provides a wide range of Internet and World Wide Web consulting services, including "search engine tune-ups," to improve a site's search engine position and ranking, Internet publicity and promotion, Web site conception and development, Web site log analysis, and general Internet training. Calafia Consulting is headed by Danny Sullivan, known widely for his work as editor of the Search Engine Watch Web site.

Caution: Some ways of promoting your listing should definitely be avoided. For those of you planning to do it yourself, see the section on "Getting a Good Search Engine Listing" in Chapter 8 for more information.

ADVERTISE IN SPECIALIZED DIRECTORIES

◆ **What are specialized directories?** These lists are simply online versions of the familiar printed yellow pages and business directories. They have several advantages over their printed counterparts. First, they can be searched with their own internal search engine.

Second, many of them include links to Web sites of listed businesses. Third, a few include photos or video listings.

Such listings also offer some advantages over the broader search engines or directories. Yellow-pages types of directories offer regional or local searches to bring meaningful, prequalified users to your listing. These directories tend to attract shoppers (not surfers) who are looking for specific information to make a buying decision. They also offer affordable, targeted advertising opportunities within your business classification and city. Better listing placement can be purchased to improve your ranking and ensure that your company listing appears in the top search results.

Business directories allow a much more focused search by a user, since unrelated topics and businesses are eliminated before the search is made. Business directory users are also prequalified, since they wouldn't be taking the time to use such a service if they didn't have a need for the business services or products being offered.

These listings have several limitations. First, only the most basic listing is available free (and with business directories, no enhanced listings are available). Second, the amount of information available to a user is restricted to name, address, and phone number (though this is changing as the directories provide more opportunity for expanded listings, video listings, or links to Web sites). Third, the online versions are less widely known, and the more selective types in particular are much harder to find online. Fourth, the vendor may restrict the frequency of listing changes.

◆ **How do I use them?** Let's start with yellow pages directories. Many yellow pages directories can be found by a search from one of the major search engines or directories. Others can be found as cross-listings on the search engines or directories. Generally, yellow pages listings are gathered under contract by one of the traditional print directories.

Yahoo! Yellow Pages (http://yp.yahoo.com) can serve as an example. Yahoo! licenses its business listings from a data provider called InfoUSA. In order for your business to have a free listing in the Yahoo! Yellow Pages, you must be included in InfoUSA's database, and your business must have a physical address (you can't simply be an online business). This also means that any updates you make to your listing will be restricted to the frequency with which the data provider updates its information (quarterly in this case).

To "enhance" your listing (add hours of operation, accepted payment methods, a link to a company Web site, and other such company information), you locate your current listing on its yellow pages site. Then you complete an online form and agree to pay $15 per month.

The services offered by the different yellow pages vendors vary widely both in price and in the types of services offered. Some associated with the search engines or sponsored by another site don't offer enhanced listings. Some offer *only* enhanced listings, and some offer full priority listings on a local, regional, and national basis. Some allow you to add your listing online, while others use an existing database and don't accept new listings except through that database. The range of services offered includes priority listing, bolder- or larger-font listings, business description lines, mini Web pages, full Web site design, e-mail link, Web site link, online map and directions, photos, and videos.

Some of the available national yellow pages directories include the following:

AT&T AnyWho Info (http://www.anywho.com/index.html) $14.95 per month ($4.95 for each additional listing)

BigYellow (http://www.bigyellow.com). [Includes America Online (Yellow Pages), GTE SuperPages, GO (Yellow Pages), Big-Book, Bell Atlantic.net (Yellow Pages), NBC Interactive Neighborhoods (Yellow Pages), AOL's Digital Cities (Yellow Pages), and The BigYellow/GTE Superpages. Networked online Yellow Pages is also accessible on a variety of popular sites, including Lycos and others.] Wide range of customized services from $20 to $5,000 per month.

CBS Switchboard.com (http://www.switchboard.com). Wide range of services available for $15 to $150 per month.

Qwest (http://www.uswestdex.com). A number of services, though not as wide as Big Yellow, from $10 to $50 per month.

The WWW Yellow Pages (http://www.yellow-pg.com) Two packages at $9.95 and $29.95.

Yellow-Page.Net (http://www.yellow-page.net) Bundled package at $150 per year.

As for business directories, since there are literally hundreds of directories available and most are free (some charge a small setup fee), the best way to evaluate them is to look for one that would appeal to your target market or that your target market would use to find you. Some examples of typical business directories are ablCOM Internet Business Directory (http://www.ablcom. com/busdir.htm), Switchboard.com (http://www.switchboard. com), and BizWeb Business Guide to the Web (http://www. bizweb.com). The best listing of links to this type of directory is Paradigm RedShift's Directory of Internet Business Directories (http://www.paradigm-redshift.com/busdir.htm). The method of sign-up varies dramatically, so you will need to investigate each one that interests you.

ADVERTISE BY JOINING AN ONLINE REFERRAL SERVICE

◆ **What are they?** An online referral is a relatively new option. Although most of the professional associations have always provided referrals to their members, effectiveness was limited because most consumers were unfamiliar with the associations or how to contact them. This situation changed with the advent of the Internet. Now many investor sites provide links to the professional association sites in answer to the question, "How do I find an adviser?" Many of the professional associations provide an online referral service on their sites. Thus, you may already be listed in the professional association site's referral service by virtue of your membership or certification.

An even more recent development are sites that offer to refer their visitors to an adviser or rep in their area. This is usually provided as part of some online financial service. A high-traffic site that prescreens advisers is MSN's Money Central's Advisor Finder (http://moneycentral.msn.com/investor/dalbar/main.asp). This new service asks consumers about their needs, preferences, and personality, and then identifies the qualified financial professionals who are best suited to provide help. Dalbar, Inc., and MSN have developed this service in conjunction with twenty-five major financial institutions.

In addition, a smaller, more focused type of site offers similar services, including prescreened free referrals. An example that emphasizes estate planning is AdvisorNet (http://www.estate planningservices.com/epsnet.htm).

A third type doesn't focus on a target market and provides no criteria for getting posted on the site. An example is fnCentral (http://fncentral.com/), which provides a suite of online budget and finance tools for the consumer. This service also allows reps to list themselves on the site with a link to the rep's Web site. Another example is Find-An-Advisor (http://www.find-an-advisor.com), which is a stand-alone service.

The QuickBooks Professional Advisors Program is a good example of the last type of site in the group. Here the focus is on developing a support service related to the adviser's core marketing. This site (http://www.quickbooks.com/banking-finance/pro advisor/) is designed to provide tools and information essential to professionals who support the small businesses that use Quick-Books software. The Certified QuickBooks ProAdvisor Program is for professional advisers who wish to achieve an exceptionally high level of QuickBooks proficiency and be recognized as a Quick-Books Specialist.

◆ **How do I use them?** In the case of the professional associations, if you are already a member and/or have achieved a special certification or recognition, the only thing you need to do is be aware of the services your organizations offer. Go to their sites and review your membership information to be sure it is current. Check that they have your e-mail and/or Web site address. This referral capability may give you an additional reason to pursue memberships or certification.

Society of Financial Service Professionals (http://www.financial pro.org/sfsp/_Consumer.html) (formerly the American Society of Chartered Life Underwriters [CLU] and Chartered Financial Consultants) will send up to five names of society members by area.

The Financial Planning Association (http://www.fpanet.org/

plannersearch/plannersearchmain.cfm) provides a list of certified financial planners by area.

The National Association of Personal Financial Advisors (NAPFA) (http://www.napfa.org/planner.htm) provides referrals to fee-only (noncommission) financial planners by state.

To be included in these referral services, you need only go to the site and apply. If you meet the criteria, you will be added. In the case of the MSN site, which is the most restrictive, you must have five years or more of experience, a clean regulatory record, a full-time practice, and a minimum number of clients (100) or amount of assets under management ($15 million). You must agree to standards of practice and service as outlined in the MS-DALBAR Professional's Guide. The service costs $750 per year, although this may be reduced by a sponsoring institution. To apply for this service contact Dalbar, Inc. (http://www.dalbar.com/Web_referral.htm), or a sponsoring institution.

ADVERTISE USING ONLINE CLASSIFIED ADS

◆ **What are they?** Classified ads in the online environment have taken on a slightly different meaning than that of traditional print classifieds. A broader array of both products and services is offered online than in print. In addition, many products and services that would normally never use a print classified ad are beginning to appear in online ads. The principal reasons for this change are the size of the potential audience, the timeliness of the ads, the ease of access, and the capability for online searches.

There are two basic types of online classified ads. Some are associated with a traditional newspaper or shopper and some are purely Web-based. Those associated with a newspaper may include joint advertising both in print and online. Those associated with traditional classifieds typically charge for their classified ads. Those that are Web-based may or may not charge.

◆ **What are they? How do I use them?** Typical of the free classified ads are those found at Yahoo! Classifieds (http://classifieds.yahoo.com). As you might imagine, the sophistication and volume of traffic to such sites varies dramatically. You also have little control over the location of potential respondents since few sites offer geographic controls. There are also posting services that will post your ads on a large number of sites that accept classified ads. An example is National Sales Services' classified ads section (http://nationalsales-services.com/Online/Classifieds/freeads.htm). The caution here is that these free ads are geared mostly to personals and selling items and not to businesses or business services. However, since they are free, you lose nothing but your time.

A better type of classified is the business or commercial classified ad. Some of these offer a display ad option allowing you to have a Web ad or Web site link. Typical of the purely online business classifieds is the MLM Classified Zone (http://worldentre.com/thezone.htm). It offers fifty- and one-hundred-word rates, from 45 to 120 days, for $10 to $29. For contrast, a typical newspaper related classified site is the *Omaha World Herald*'s Classified section (http://www.omaha.com). In this instance, there is no online method of adding an ad. Many newspapers do offer that feature, and the rates (which, of course, you should check) for the printed classified automatically include the online version as well. Rates vary according to the newspaper's circulation and/or site traffic.

There are two ways to approach this type of advertising. Since you should be familiar with the papers in your area, you can simply do a search on the paper or shopper's name. Most papers of any size have a Web site, and most offer online or joint classified ads (though, as in the case of the World Herald, you may need to call for rates). The other approach is to go to a supersite that will allow you to place ads with multiple papers and online classifieds. This is the best way to find purely online business classifieds since there is no uniformity in their site names, so a great number overlap with the free classified sites. A good example of a supersite is Advertise 123 (http://www.advertise123.com).

ADVERTISE USING ONLINE INFORMATIONAL SEMINARS

◆ **What are they?** An informational seminar's purpose is to present information on a topic that the prospect values. Then you must impress the prospect with your expertise. Your card and product/service materials are left in a prominent location in the hope that the prospect will wish to engage you as a representative.

An online version of the approach has the same purpose. However, rather than leaving your card and materials to pique interest, you place a link to your Web site in a prominent place on the online seminar site.

◆ **How do I use them?** These seminars are identical in structure and online support needs to the online sales seminars described earlier.

ADVERTISE USING WEB SITE SPONSORSHIP

◆ **What is this?** Another type of Internet advertising is sponsorship. Here, rather than purchasing an ad, you help "sponsor" the site. This usually means helping the site owner pay the costs of maintaining the site. However, another option for those with a substantial Web presence is to host the site on your site.

◆ **How do I use it?** Since you don't have a traditional ad with which to intrigue a potential prospect (sponsorship is usually acknowledged at the bottom of the home page or on a special sponsors page), this form of advertising is a better choice for "image" advertising. Quite a few site owners will allow a link from the sponsored site to your site.

If used properly, this approach can become a powerful relationship-building tool. It is especially useful for supporting local nonprofit, charitable, or religious Web sites.

ADVERTISE BY WRITING FOR WEB SITES

◆ **What is this?** Everyone realizes that the Internet is growing at an incredible rate. What you may not realize is that this explosive growth has created a huge content gap. Businesses are slapping up Web sites only to find that there is no one to write the articles they need to keep fresh content available. Most freelance authors are unwilling to take these assignments since they pay very little (or nothing). This means a Web site owner is always on the lookout for new authors.

This presents an opportunity for you. Since you are more interested in developing new customers than in getting paid a living wage for writing, you can leverage your expertise by writing for these sites. At first blush, you may think that your expertise is too narrow. However, the reality is that there are many aspects of financial planning, investing, the markets, and related topics that a surprising number of sites would be interested in.

◆ **How do I go about this?** Remember that your broker-dealer considers this an outside business activity, so you will need to make him aware of what you're planning. Since you are most interested in developing a local reputation, the best place to start is with local Web sites. Several types of sites might be interested in articles about financial services.

The first type is the city portal site. Any search engine will provide you with a list of city- and county-related Web sites. Some of these will be governmental and some private—look at both types. Focus on your own town and nearby cities, and browse the pages to see what kind of writing they have on their sites. Then develop an outline for an article, along with a series of future topics. As you develop your outline, remember that this is not a sales pitch, so use a simple concept, keep your article factual, and make it light and entertaining. Contact the Web editor with an inquiry and attach your article and series outlines. Be sure you indicate that you would be willing to contribute your articles for only nominal compensation (or for free) as long as your Web site link is included.

Another type of site to approach is the local online newsmagazine, which usually has a low budget and is willing to take a chance on an unknown—especially if you do not require much compensation. You can also try the online version of your local paper. Although a large-circulation daily is unlikely to accept your material, many smaller papers are willing to allow outside writers.

Try nonprofit sites. Many charities deal with people who have had financial problems and need help in developing budgets and savings plans. Remember that many of the people who visit these sites are the contributors who help fund the charity.

If you are more ambitious, you can approach a larger site that caters to regional or national audiences. The tactic here is a bit different from writing for a local site. Here your purpose is to build up your reputation so you can leverage this expertise in your other marketing.

There are several ways to find a larger site that might publish your article. First, simply think of a topic that you would like to write about, and then do a search using that topic as the keyword. Check out the links you locate. If a site already has an article on a similar topic, chances are good that it would be interested in related articles. To verify that a site has sufficient traffic to be worth investing your time and effort, do several searches on topics related to the site's core purpose. See if this site appears repeatedly. If it does, chances are good that this site has brisk traffic. (See also the earlier section on "Internet Advertising" in this chapter.)

Look at portal, search, or directory sites that create their own content. A good example is About.com (http://home.about .com/index.htm). The following directory site uses outside experts (or authors) to organize and write about different topics: (http:// expertcentral.com/why/).

TRADITIONAL PASSIVE MARKETING GOES ONLINE

JUST AS WITH TRADITIONAL active marketing, traditional approaches to passive marketing can be made much more efficient by using online resources. I mentioned business directories earlier with regard to advertising. They aren't the only vehicle for using these services. The Internet is a very effective way to develop niche or target marketing information. Part One of this book goes into some of the sources for niche marketing information, so I won't repeat those here. However, there is a wealth of this type of targeted marketing information online.

Use an Internet business directory to identify a list of specific business types in your area. For example, you could look for all the CPAs located close to your office. Then send a letter or e-mail inviting them to a seminar. Earlier I mentioned ablCOM Internet Business Directory (http://www.ablcom.com/busdir.htm) and BizWeb Business Guide to the Web (http://www.bizweb.com). Another excellent site is Switchboard.com (http://www.switchboard.com). Use the listing of business directory links at Paradigm RedShift's Directory of Internet Business Directories (http://www.paradigm -redshift.com/busdir.htm) to find more.

If you exhibit in trade shows as part of your marketing approach, you will be interested to know that the Trade Show News Network (http://tsnn.com) allows you to locate shows by industry, month, location, or trade show name. You can also search for other exhibitors or suppliers. You can find a similar listing for associations at the American Society of Association Executives (http://www.asaenet.org).

If you like to target home owners, use Yahoo! Real Estate (http://realestate.yahoo.com) or REALTOR.com (http://www.realtor.com/) to determine home prices and which homes have recently sold in your area.

Another way to use the Web to enhance your traditional marketing is to look for software or Internet-based applications. Obviously, there are hundreds of applications available online; however, a well-designed search will usually discover what you are looking for. Software ranges from traditional contact managers such as Goldmine (http://goldmine.com) or ACT! (http://act.com) to mapping software like ESRI (http://www.esri.com) to map both the demographics and locations of your current client database.

Staying in Touch with Your Clients (Sales Support)

PART ONE OF THIS BOOK delves into a client-service marketing strategy. There I discuss a number of ways both to provide service and to generate new sales from your existing clients. Here I will go into a bit more detail on some client sales and service tools and discuss some other effective approaches.

E-MAIL CLIENT SALES AND SERVICE

THE INTERNET DOES PROVIDE you with a unique and personal way to stay in touch with your clients. It also provides you an efficient means to increase your client sales. So this means you jump on the Internet and e-mail all your clients, right? Wrong! The Internet is a communications channel, one of many you can choose. E-mail is only one of the tools available in this channel. Like any tool, it only works well if you take the time to learn how to use it. You must approach all your online client contacts carefully and with a plan, or you run the risk of alienating your clients.

◆ **What is it?** E-mail sales to current clients uses the same techniques as described earlier in "Direct E-mail Marketing," Chapter 3. The only real difference is that you already have an implied permission from your clients to contact them periodically to inform them of opportunities. This is sufficient for most other forms of marketing, but the rules governing e-mail are a bit foggy due to concerns over spamming. It may be wise to obtain explicit permission for e-mail follow-up at the time of your initial sale.

E-mail service can be much more than simply sending your client a reminder to mail in that form. E-mail contacts can be integrated with your service schedule. One option is to install software that automates your e-mail contacts based on a calendar of events personalized by client. This may require a bit of data entry and/or manual steps, however, since only a few contact management systems include an automated e-mail function.

However, an even better solution is what some broker-dealers are developing: a fully integrated online client management system that includes both back-office and front-office functions. Such a system will allow you to seamlessly automate e-mails to remind clients of upcoming service events.

Another option is to create your own client e-zine (or e-mail newsletter). Depending on the length, the newsletter can be the e-mail, summary paragraphs with links back to your site for details, or a single link back to a PDF or HTML newsletter that fully resides on your site.

◆ **How do I use it?** Examples of online contact managers that allow automated e-mails include Focus Internet Service's Twig (http://www.focus.lu/hosting/extensions/twig/index.html) and Management Software, Inc.'s Uptrends (http://www.uptrends .com/html/products_actionmgr_additional.html). Other familiar contact management systems such as Symantec's ACT! and Goldmine's Front Office are sure to follow. However, even when you can't fully automate the e-mail process, e-mail contacts are still much more efficient since you can create a single e-mail and instantly send it to whichever clients you indicate—no printing, no postage, no time delay. It arrives the same day it is sent.

You can even embed links to an automated sales presentation

that you can create using a simple Microsoft PowerPoint software program and then post on your site. This allows you to be very creative in what you send, yet still keep the e-mail itself very short.

It is even possible to include forms that the client can complete online and return to you. Where a signature is necessary, the form can be printed by the client, then signed and sent to you. This can be a great time-saver and reduce your need to store so many forms in your office. You can convert the form to a PDF file using Adobe Acrobat. Another option under Adobe allows the client to complete the form's fields online. You may even find that your broker-dealer already provides some or all of its forms in PDF versions.

PDF is also useful for displaying color brochures or other marketing materials. One caution: Some of these graphic files can be quite large, and if they are not optimized properly, they will take a very long time to download. A good graphic-image studio can help you create a PDF file that opens as efficiently as possible. However, be sure you test the file from a remote location after you post it to see how long it takes to download.

RELATIONSHIP-BUILDING ONLINE

KIP GREGORY OF THE GREGORY GROUP has developed an excellent "12 Step" program to help you work with the Web to build better relationships.[6]

For many advisers, the toughest challenge in leveraging the Internet is not knowing where to begin. To get you started, here's a step-by-step approach for using the Web to stay close to clients and other important contacts, using the strategies, tactics, and tools described below:

1 Next time you're talking with key clients or top prospects about the Web, ask (or listen) for their favorite site(s). Find out what they like and use the most at each one. Jot down the answers: They're the "information posts" you'll use to build a fence around the relationship.

2 Upgrade your Web browser to Microsoft Internet Explorer (IE) v5.5. Call 877-676-1120 to request a CD or download it at http://www.microsoft.com/windows/ie/default. You'll need IE to use some of the tools mentioned below.

3 Create a Favorites folder for each key contact in IE, then book-mark (save to Favorites) sites they've mentioned; alphabetize the list of bookmarks for easy scanning.

4 Open accounts at http://www.blink.com for yourself and each key contact; import or copy the list of Favorites from your PC to Blink. Be sure to browse Blink's directory for other sites of interest in their categories.

5 Use IE's "Show Related Links" (on the Tools menu) to locate sites similar to those favorites; add the worthwhile ones to Blink.

6 If key contacts don't already have one, build a customized start page for each using his preferred portal—Yahoo!, Excite, etc. Por-tals are usually search engine sites, although some high-traffic sites and targeted commercial sites also offer portals. See Appendix B for a more complete listing of major search engines and directories.

7 Notify contacts by e-mail that you've created a personal start page and bookmark account for them on the Web and invite them to call your office to arrange a "tour." Follow up with a phone call a few days later to reiterate your offer.

8 Open an account at iHarvest (http://www.iharvest.com/) to create a filing cabinet of important Web content. You'll use some unique features of iHarvest later.

9 Scour files, client profiles, and records for ideas on what to share with your key group. Create a list of five to ten topic cate-gories to select from when sharing information with each person. Use that list to create a communications strategy and schedule. Plan to send at least one useful article to them monthly for the next year.

10 Use one or more of the major search engines (see Appendix B) and WebFerret (http://www.ferretsoft.com/netferret/index .html) to search for relevant Web content. WebFerret is actually software you download. The advantages of WebFerret are that you can do Boolean searches (if, and, or, not, etc.) across multiple search engines, remove duplicate listings, do searches in the back-ground, sort, and save the results to your desktop. When you find a site you like, bookmark it in your Blink account. Consider setting up a subscription to sites you visit often using IE's "Make available offline" feature in the "Add to favorites" feature.

11 Annotate, highlight, and save selected Web pages to your iHarvest account. This allows you to personalize the pages you send to your clients in the next step.

12 Send yourself an e-mail from iHarvest with links to each article to be sent. Edit the message you receive to delete the iHarvest promotional copy. Write a brief message to key contacts and forward it, using mailing list groups set up in your e-mail or contact management program.

Don't forget: Coach your clients on how to use these tools themselves!

CHAPTER

WHAT MAKES A GOOD SITE GOOD?

LET'S SAY YOU ARE LOOKING at some examples of a Web developer's work. They all look terrific. Yet, how do you know when you're looking at a great site? What makes it great? What do the site's creators know that you don't? All good sites follow some basic guidelines. Here are some tips on what your developer should do and avoid doing when building your site. Most of these tips apply to custom sites, with which there is greater control over the site design, though most tips can be used to help you evaluate the work of template developers.

In addition, we'll look at why you should have a professional review your site. This is a good idea even when you had another professional build your site for you. Finally, if you would like to look at some really good sites just for ideas, or if you feel you have developed a really

Do's

◆ DO KISS (Keep It Simple, Stupid!).
◆ DO be sure your design encourages repeat traffic.
◆ DO update your Web pages often.
◆ DO copyright any content you develop.
◆ DO include your contact information.
◆ DO test your site with different browsers.
◆ DO determine the browser your visitors are using.
◆ DO have download links for any required plug-ins.
◆ DO be sure your site navigation is simple to use.
◆ DO use graphics to brighten up your pages.
◆ DO be consistent with your art.
◆ DO use photos sparingly.
◆ DO use animation very, very sparingly.
◆ DO use white (or light) backgrounds for text.
◆ DO use dark backgrounds for photographs.
◆ DO use color coding as a navigation cue.
◆ DO minimize the use of italic fonts.
◆ DO use lead-ins, subheads, and lift paragraphs to break up large blocks of type.
◆ DO break up your text headings into multiple Web pages.
◆ DO organize your text into columns.
◆ DO keep your spacing consistent!
◆ DO progressively render graphics and text to give the impression of faster downloading.

"hot" site, I'll introduce you to some of the companies that rate sites and give site awards.

The chart above[1] summarizes the do's and don'ts of having a Web site developed. When you evaluate Web developers, look at samples of their work, and, of course, look critically at your own site, both initially and periodically. Use this list to prepare a thorough assessment. Many of the items are particularly useful in helping you prepare content you would like your developer to post on

Don'ts

- ◆ DON'T put barriers between visitors and content.
- ◆ DON'T change your site format frequently.
- ◆ DON'T use icons alone for navigation.
- ◆ DON'T violate generally accepted guidelines for Web site design.
- ◆ DON'T use large graphics or a large number of graphics on a single page.
- ◆ DON'T use video clips.
- ◆ DON'T use slow-loading sound clips.
- ◆ DON'T ever include rapidly repeating animation.
- ◆ DON'T use highly textured backgrounds behind text.
- ◆ DON'T overprint type on a colored background or reverse type out of a light-colored background.
- ◆ DON'T overuse type attributes like bold, color, blinking, etc.— less is more!
- ◆ DON'T use all caps unless you're shouting!
- ◆ DON'T use underlines except in special cases.
- ◆ DON'T use more than two different typefaces in a given document.
- ◆ DON'T try to cram too much material onto a page—make good use of white space.
- ◆ DON'T load the top portion of the page with large graphics— this prevents text from loading.

your site, since a developer is unlikely to act as your editor. Each of these do's and don'ts is organized by category and covered in greater detail in the sections that follow.

Do's and Don'ts, in General

DO REMEMBER THE OLD ACRONYM *KISS*: "Keep it simple, stupid!" Don't substitute design dazzle for content. Web visitors come to a site because they need what's on the site or because they're interested in learning something about what the site offers. Either way, they want to know—and quickly—what's on your site. Anything that doesn't educate them or inform them about your products or services wastes bandwidth!

Don't let your developer put barriers between visitors and content. Page design and layout can play a major role in keeping or losing visitors. The harder it is for visitors to find what you have on your site, the more frustrated they get and the more likely they will leave your Web site.

Do be sure your site's design encourages repeat traffic. Whether your site is designed for sales, service, or both, unless it has something the visitor wants, it's not worth your effort.

Do update your Web pages frequently. Even if your site builds great return traffic, that traffic will dwindle rapidly if the return visitor sees the same information again and again.

Do copyright your work. If you develop significant original content for your site, protect that content and the time you invested in writing it with a copyright.

Do include your contact information. It sounds as if I'm stating the obvious, but it can be easy to overlook. If you're dealing with a template site, this isn't as much of a problem since that is usually included as part of the template. However, with custom site developers it can get missed. No matter how excited a potential prospect might be, if there is no way to phone, fax, or e-mail you, your site is a wasted effort.

BROWSERS AND PLUG-INS

DO TEST YOUR SITE with different browsers. They do not all work the same. Even if your developer assures you your site will work with any browser, test it! If it doesn't work correctly, make sure the developer fixes it. By testing, you eliminate nasty surprises for your site's visitors. Generally, they will not give you a second chance if your site does not work properly when they first visit.

Do determine which Web browser (and which version) visitors to your Web site are using. If, because of some functional limitation, your developer selects a single browser (or browser version) as the preferred browser, then let the user know immediately. Make sure the developer provides browser download links, so the visitor can download the necessary browser(s) from your site.

Do make sure your developer provides download links for any special software plug-ins the user may need to properly view your site, such as Adobe Acrobat Reader, Shockwave, and so on.

FORMAT AND NAVIGATION

DON'T CHANGE YOUR FORMAT within the site once it is established. Template site developers periodically introduce new layout or navigation templates. Resist the temptation to change to the new template just because it is new. If you have a custom site, it is easy to get carried away with the latest "cool" look. Custom developers love modifications (more revenue!). Once the visitor has figured out how to find things on your site, it is very distracting and annoying to have it suddenly change.

Do be sure your developer's layout contains links back up the hierarchy, not just the "back" button on your browser.

Don't use icons alone on custom sites (template sites usually dictate icon usage). Studies show that the user most often does not understand icons—it is better to "cheat" and insert a word under the icon than to leave the user to guess its meaning.

PHOTOS AND GRAPHICS

DON'T ALLOW YOUR DEVELOPER to violate generally accepted guidelines for Web site design concerning such aspects as the foreground, middle ground, and background of a Web page. Too many Web site designers put the wrong design elements in the wrong part of the page. If it looks "funny" to you or your site visitors, it is probably wrong.

Do make sure your custom site designer uses clip art and other graphics to brighten up your pages, but doesn't go crazy with such art. The old "too much of a good thing" adage definitely applies here.

Do be consistent with your art. Cartoonish clip art may clash with straightforward line drawings or illustrations when used on the same page or in the same section. This is particularly a problem when you are providing content that already includes graphics.

Make sure that the art you are including is consistent with the existing site template or layout. It's usually obvious even to nondesigners when art styles don't blend well.

Don't include a large graphics illustration or a large number of individual graphics on a single page unless they can be reduced in resolution to around 72 dpi (or optimized). Otherwise, your pages will take much too long to download. Again, the principal culprits here are the articles or newsletters you have inserted on your site. Just because it looks good in print does not mean it will work online. Remember that the average visitor will only wait a few seconds for a page to load. If it takes longer than twenty seconds, they will click to another site.

Do use photos sparingly and only if they are of good quality. Remember, a photo tour of your office might be good for your ego but will probably drive visitors away. Any photos you do place on your site need to be reduced in resolution to around 72 dpi (or optimized) so they load quickly.

SOUND OR VIDEO

DON'T HAVE YOUR custom site developer use video clips unless your target market has high-bandwidth Internet access. This is usually not the case with most financial service prospects.

Don't have your custom site developer use sound clips that take too long to download. Sound should be used sparingly and should never play continuously as background (this can become very annoying). Make sure that the clip can be turned off from your site and terminates automatically when the visitor leaves your site.

ANIMATION

DO HAVE YOUR custom site developer use animation very, very sparingly. Moving images have an overpowering effect on the eye, making it very difficult for readers to concentrate on reading the text.

Don't ever have your custom site developer include permanently moving animation on a Web page. Animations should stop after a limited number of repeats—two or three at most.

BACKGROUNDS

DO HAVE YOUR custom site developer use white (or light) backgrounds for text. The greatest contrast (black on white) provides the highest readability.

Do have your custom site developer use very dark backgrounds for multiple photographs and a gallerylike effect.

Don't have your custom site developer use highly textured backgrounds behind text since they can substantially reduce readability.

COLOR

DO HAVE YOUR custom site developer use color coding as a secondary navigation cue. Do not let your custom site developer overprint type on a colored background or reverse type out of a colored block. For example, light blue type on a dark blue or black background is too hard to read. Type reversed out of a background should be in a very light color or, preferably, white. Strong, bold, sans-serif faces work best.

NOTE: THE NEXT TWO SECTIONS are particularly important in evaluating articles and newsletters before sending them to the site developer for placement on your site. Your developer will not edit your content.

FONT

DON'T OVERUSE type attributes such as bold, blinking, color, and contrast. When all of these elements are added to a page, they overwhelm the reader and negate each individual attribute. Again, less is more.

Don't use all caps UNLESS YOU WANT TO SHOUT AT THE READER!

Don't use underlines except in very special cases. Underlining is a holdover from the days when it was one of the few means to emphasize words or phrases with typewriters. Now we can use boldface or small caps for emphasis. Underlines are also used extensively for hyperlinks and can be confusing if used where there is no link.

Do minimize the use of italic fonts, because they are difficult to read on a computer monitor. Italic fonts are at complete odds with the constraints of a square pixel grid, usually look bad, and guarantee degraded readability.

Don't use more than two different typefaces in a given document or publication. For variety, use different sizes (ten, twelve, or fourteen point), weights (light, regular, bold, or heavy), and styles (normal or roman, italic, bold, small and drop caps). Experts often recommend using a serif face (such as Times Roman or Garamond) for body copy and a sans-serif face (such as Helvetica or Arial) for headlines, subheads, and captions. But use your common sense when applying this rule online, since small serif fonts (ten point or smaller) can be hard to read on a monitor. For those of you using a template Web site, take the time to find out the typeface being used on your site so you can match it when you create content.

TEXT

DO USE LEAD-INS, subheads, and lift-out paragraphs (sometimes called "pull quotes") liberally to break up large blocks of type. Subheads and short summaries or lead-ins can provide a transition between headlines and body copy. Subheads also break up body text into sections and identify the subject of those sections. Lift paragraphs consist of text pulled from the body copy and placed in a screened box or between rules, usually in a font heavier or otherwise distinct from the body type, to break up a "gray" or text-heavy page. Be careful how you place pull quotes online since the text will wrap differently on different monitors, resolutions, and browsers. Avoid letting the pull quote float with the text or placing it too far to the left. It may end up in an awkward location on the page or require you to scroll in order to see it.

Do break up your text headings into multiple Web pages. Many subheads can become their own pages with a link from the main page. If possible, avoid causing the visitor to have to scroll down the page to finish the text. Very long Web pages tend to be disorienting. But be cautious in the use of multiple page links. This type of page is more difficult to maintain and should be avoided if an entire section is updated frequently. It is more appropriate when the subsection's content changes but the subsection headings remain constant (a newsletter with monthly columns would be a good example).

Do organize your text into columns. The muscles controlling the eye during reading tire sooner when they are subjected to long lengths of text. Although text-heavy pages are not recommended, it is less strenuous to read them if the text is constrained to a few inches in width. Your developer (even template site developers) can do this for you in most cases if you request it.

Don't try to cram too much material onto a page. White (or negative) space is a valuable design tool; use it well. That means allowing adequate margins and gutters (the space between columns) as well as leading (space between lines).

Do keep your spacing consistent! Uneven spacing between heads and body copy, or between paragraphs, can be distracting to a reader.

DOWNLOADING CONSIDERATIONS

DO HAVE YOUR custom developer use progressive rendering of graphics and text to give the impression of faster downloading and to mask the time delay. It helps if the user can start reading the page while parts of the screen are still rendering.

Don't let your custom developer load the top portion of the page with large graphics. Keeping this area free allows the visitor to start reading the page while the more serious downloading is happening out of sight.

FINDING GOOD SITES

IF YOU WANT TO SEE what a good Web site looks like, go look at some award-winning sites or a site that has received excellent write-ups. Seeing what others have done can be a very good source of ideas for developing your own site (even if the site's mission is completely different from your own).

What follows is a sampling of Web awards and reviews. The first few awards are for larger commercial sites and are included here primarily for comparison purposes—giving you a standard against which to compare your site. Then look at the award winners from the other award sites. Print pages that contain layout or function ideas you like. Take notes on these pages to indicate the specific ideas that appealed to you, because later you may forget why you printed the page.

◆ **Cool Site of the Day!** (http://cool.infi.net)

◆ **Imagine Success Award Program's Eagle Has Landed Award** (http://www.imaginesuccess.com/award.html)

◆ **The Best of the Planet** (http://www.2ask.com)

◆ **The IPPA Award for Design Excellence**, also known as the DX, sets the standard for commercial design on the Internet (http://www.ippa.org/main.html)

◆ **The JBS Business Site Award** (http://freeweb.pdq.net/childress/award/award.htm)

◆ **World Best Web Site** (http://www.worldbestWeb site.com/default.htm)

◆ **Yahoo! Internet Life and ZDNet's Gold Star Personal Finance site** (http://www.zdnet.com/techlife/)

If you want to look at a bigger range of award sites, go to http://www.awardsites.com. This free promotional service offers rating levels, graphic/text links to the award site, and descriptions for Web site awards and reviews. There are eight rating levels ranging from one to five and even special categories for specific types of awards.

Content of a Typical Rep Site

THERE IS AN INCREDIBLE RANGE of content available for Web sites on financial services. In this section, we'll look at the content found in most typical representative sites. Most of this information should appear somewhere in almost any rep site. Specialized content suggestions are found in the "Building Specialized Niche Sites" section (page 135). Always keep in mind that your marketing strategy drives the content of your site. Don't add content simply because you think it is interesting or you see it on someone else's site. If the content isn't consistent with your strategy, it should not be on your site!

PREPACKAGED CONTENT AND FUNCTIONS

VENDORS THAT SPECIALIZE in developing and/or hosting rep or adviser sites have customized the features and packaged the cost of most types of online content and tools (like those described below) in the site's hosting cost. What is available will vary from vendor to vendor. Some of the functions and content may even be unique to a particular developer.

Template site developers are particularly likely to offer specialized features. Template developers will normally be the most restrictive in allowing outside content and functions to be added to their sites. Most will allow links from their template site to another vendor, but few will fully integrate this outside content into their site. So while you can add the outside content and functions, they will not look like they are part of your site. This is a factor when choosing a site developer.

If you want to seamlessly integrate content and functions from a number of outside vendors into a single site, you need to select a custom site developer. The functions or content from any of the vendors mentioned in the following sections could be fully integrated into a custom site.

We will look at the template and custom site developer options in more detail in Chapter 7, "Web Site Developers."

As you review the content suggestions below, you will see the term "sponsored" or "partners" used. This refers to those vendors that allow you to co-brand a site's content and link it to your site. This can be useful. However, the information on a partner's site doesn't reside on your Web site. Be sure the site you link to is very simple and narrow in scope. It should not have links that allow the visitor to surf off to some other site. Be sure also that returning to your site is easy and seamless (not just having the visitor click on the back button). It is very easy for a visitor to get lost in a partner's site and never return to your site if the navigation isn't clear.

Caution: All the information suggested here must be approved by your compliance department before it appears on your site. For compliance purposes, it is also an excellent idea to have an initial screen appear that provides a list of those states in which you are licensed and what licenses you hold. Remember that your visitors could be coming from anywhere in the world. Neither you nor they would appreciate spending a lot of time discussing investments you're not licensed to sell.

REP INFORMATION

ON YOUR SITE, you will need to include your name, address, zip, phone, fax, and e-mail (include your cell phone number or second line, if applicable). You will want to be sure you include any professional designations you've earned (CFA, CFP, CLU, CFS, ChFC, CPA, MSFS, J.D., etc.). List your licenses (securities and life), and if you are a registered investment adviser, include that information as well.

You will want to work up a personal biography. As you write this, remember who your target audience is and tailor the information you include to appeal to that audience. Your purpose is to make the prospect or client comfortable with your knowledge and experience. If you have received any awards or special recognition, mention them here. Mention any specialties, such as 401(k), 403(b), equities, life, annuities, small business retirement or benefit plans, high net worth, and so on. If you are an investment adviser, indicate whether you specialize in money management, asset allocation, retirement planning, financial planning, estate planning, or some other advisory specialty.

If you are under an office of supervisory jurisdiction (OSJ), you will need to list the office name, address, and phone. Give information for each registered representative in your office (possibly your office assistants, particularly if they are registered). Remember those reps' prospects and clients will want to find out about their rep's background.

COMPANY OR FIRM INFORMATION

IF YOUR OFFICE CONTAINS more than one registered principal, has its own identity within your community, is highly specialized, or is simply very large, you may want to include a section about the firm. This section should briefly describe the firm's history and successes. Your purpose here is similar to the biography. You want to make the prospect or client comfortable with the firm's experience and in-house expertise. Any recognition the firm has received should be included. List and explain the firm's specialties. If the firm has a mission statement or a value statement, include it here. If your firm is large enough to have specialized departments, you should include an organization chart. Include a client list (with contact information) if appropriate.

You will need to include your firm's name, address, zip, phone, fax, and e-mail. If your firm does business under more than one DBA, include these other names, unless that business is unrelated. Try to avoid duplicating information in this section and the personal biographies.

FINANCIAL TOOLS

YOU CAN PURCHASE a number of online calculators, concept presentations, and financial planning tools for your site. Most financial Web site specialist developers have a selection of relevant financial tools, but they may not have exactly what you are looking for. Take time to look at what is available online. Adding a unique tool to your site will help differentiate it from the crowd. These tools range in both sophistication and cost. Such tools can be added to most template sites with a simple link and fully integrated with a custom site.

Many of these tools (particularly calculators) are sponsored and may be available free elsewhere on the Web. However, purchased (or freestanding) tools have the advantage of residing on and being fully integrated with your site. Even with a template site, you can host a tool on your own mini site (see Chapter 1 for more information on mini sites). Remember that any link to another's site allows a potential prospect or client to leave your site. This reduces the value of your site and increases the likelihood that the visitor will simply go directly to the linked site and bypass you in the future.

CALCULATORS

THERE ARE MANY SOURCES for online calculators. At the free/low-cost and less sophisticated end of the spectrum are such sites as Hugh's Mortgage and Financial Calculators (http://www.interest.com/hugh/calc/) and Web Winder (http://www.webwinder.com/wwhtmbin/javacalc.html). Quicken.com's tools and the FinanCenter, Inc., calculators are also available under a co-branding agreement (http://www.quicken.com/affiliates/

notemplates/tools.html and http://www.financenterinc.com/ products/products.html). The Hedgehog's Calculators are available for license to other sites. You need to contact them to discuss pricing (http://www.hedge-hog.com/sub/calculators.html).

TimeValue Software includes more sophisticated (and, of course, more costly) calculators (http://www.tcalc.com/ tcalcbody.asp). Financial Calculators, KJE Computer Solutions, and Brentmark Software also offer more sophisticated and expensive calculators (http://www.fincalc.com/), (http://www.dinkytown. net), and (http://www.calctools.com). Web Dynamics offers a number of general insurance and securities-related calculators (http://www.myfrontdoor.com/tools.html). AdvisorLinks (http:// www.advisorlinks.com) also offers insurance calculators. Clearview Software offers a Java Applet called the Internet Retirement Assessor (IRA) for online 401(k) support (http://www.javasoft.com/ javareel/isv/Clearview/index.htm).

Martindale's Calculators On-Line Center is a massive compendium of calculators available for sale from various sites. This site covers more than just financial calculators, so you need to surf around a bit to find what you need (http://www-sci.lib.uci. edu/HSG/RefCalculators.html).

CONCEPT PRESENTATIONS

CONCEPT PRESENTATIONS DISPLAY an idea or statistic in a compelling, short, visually oriented manner. They may be identical to the printed or slide materials that you use to explain a concept to your prospects or clients. These presentations can be static or interactive. Caution: Be sure you check with the publisher before you post its copyrighted material on your site. The company may have special Internet pricing, so just because you purchased a copy of its printed material does not mean you are authorized to post it on your Web site.

Some of these materials are Internet-ready and require only that you post them on your site. However, some were not specifically designed for online use. If you are not sure, ask the developer for permission to use the content online. The content could be in the form of files, printed pages, or slides. In the case of files, check the resolution. Anything higher than 72 dpi will need to be optimized for Internet use. Printed material and slides can usually be scanned into a file and then placed online.

401Kafe.com furnishes you with a range of investment content—from the very basics of 401(k) investing to a more advanced course in financial economics (http://www.401kafe.com/partners/partners.html). Ibbotson Presentation Materials, CDA Wiesenberger Page Charts, and Standard & Poor's Advisor Insight Client Communications provide static charts, graphs, and concept discussions that could be adapted for online use (http://www.ibbotson.com/Products/product_presentations.asp), (http://www.advisorinsight.com/ai/preview/index.htm).

ONLINE FINANCIAL PLANNING TOOLS (FOR REGISTERED INVESTMENT ADVISERS ONLY)

A NUMBER OF financial planning software firms either have or are building online platforms. Some of these can be integrated into your Web site. The capabilities of these Web site systems vary widely. Some have no program yet, others collect only basic information or give simplified plans, and still others have a more robust planning function. Some are designed only for rep use, others for joint client/rep use, and still others for client-only use. The keys to evaluating these systems for use on a rep Web site are (1) Are they user-friendly? (2) Do they load quickly? (3) Do they collect a level of information that you are comfortable with? (4) Is the output detailed enough? (5) Will it download the information collected into its own software? These last three are, in part, a personal choice.

It would be wise to monitor the key players in this area since this type of Internet development is moving rapidly. Here are some of the more popular financial planning vendors:

◆ **The Advisors Edge** (http://www.theadvisorsedge.com) offers the Web-based Private Limited Access Center, but nothing yet for consumers.

◆ **Centerpiece** (http://www.centerpiece.com) contains an eReports feature that lets you easily export reports from Centerpiece so they can be published on a Web site.

◆ **Financeware.com** (http://fplanauditors.com/default.asp) has a suite of software for Web site support, including fplanauditors. com, a comprehensive joint client/rep online financial planning software package.

◆ **Financial Profiles** (http://www.profiles.com) is an online and less robust version of the Profiles+ software, available as part of the Profiles Online rep Web site package.

◆ **First Financial Software** (http://www.fplan.com) currently has no rep Web site version.

◆ **LifeGoals Corporation** (http://www.lifegoals.com) provides rep Web site development support and integration with the company's LGX planning software.

◆ **Lumen Systems, Inc.** (http://www.lumensystems.com) offers their Web-based NorthStar system, but nothing yet for consumers.

◆ **Mobius Group** (http://www.mobiusg.com) currently has no rep Web site version.

◆ **Money Tree Software** (http://www.moneytree.com) currently has no rep Web site version.

◆ **NetDecide** (http://www.netdecide.com/html/home.htm) provides integrated software for comprehensive joint client/rep online financial planning. Includes back-office integration. Designed primarily for larger firms or broker-dealers.

◆ **Sungard Expert Solutions** (http://www.expert.sungard.com) offers an entire system that is Internet ready.

MARKET DATA

MARKET DATA CONSIST OF such things as detailed stock quotes (usually delayed, though some real-time figures are available), charting, symbol search, news tickers, earnings estimates, etc. The data can be seamlessly integrated with your site. Again, this discourages visitors from leaving your site to enter a new site. Some stock market data is available free and some for a fee.

◆ **Chartist Pro** provides very sophisticated charting capability for a fee (http://www.chartistpro.com/ie5.html).

◆ **PCQuote.com** offers a robust collection of fee-based market data (http://www.pcquote.com/business/webtemplates/index.php).

◆ **ProphetFinance.com** provides free cobranded charting pages for your Web site (http://www.prophetfinance.com/aboutprophet/sca.html).

◆ **RealTime Quotes** provides a range of products including full streaming real-time quotes (http://www.rtquotes.com).

◆ **Stockcodes.com** is a site designed for Webmasters, but it has a number of useful market data tools (nearly all are free). The downside is that some require knowledge of HTML to integrate with your site. The most useful sections of the site have free market data from a number of Web sites (http://www.stockcodes.com/partner.htm). The site also has various free Java tickers that provide updated news, stock market results (http://www.stockcodes.com/java.htm), earnings estimates (http://www.stockcodes.com/estimates.htm), and delayed stock quotes (http://www.stockcodes.com/quotes.htm).

◆ **TickerTech.com** offers, for a fee, versions of the JavaTicker, News Ticker, and Investor Ticker designed for use by other sites (http://www.javaticker.com/products/).

◆ **World Wide Quote** offers real-time and delayed quotes along with other market data services from exchanges worldwide (http://www.wwquote.com).

LIFE, ANNUITY, AND MUTUAL FUND INFORMATION

NEARLY EVERY INSURANCE COMPANY or mutual fund has a Web site. However, you need to be careful in creating links from your site to the fund or carrier site. Few of these sites have a section specifically designed to support a link from a rep Web site. Such a site or section of a site has to be carefully designed to reinforce the role of the rep/adviser in providing advice and/or service.

Unfortunately, some companies have specifically designed their sites to promote direct fund, insurance, or annuity sales through the company (in some instances online). If you are not careful, you could find yourself making the sale but getting nothing for it. Even if you avoid this problem, most company sites promote their entire product line. This may include products that are not approved for sale by your broker-dealer.

Review the company's site carefully before you place a link on your site. Your compliance department can be of help here; they can look at the site and tell you if it is appropriate for a link (they may even have already reviewed it). You also should check with your broker-dealer to see which products are on the approved product list.

Another option is to integrate fund or annuity information from the main content providers. An example is Morningstar's Quicktakes Plus program, which allows you to choose what content you want from the information on their site (http://www.morningstar.com/products/coqp.html). The advantage is that a large number of products can be reviewed quickly, without going through a number of unfamiliar company sites with different navigation and layout. The main disadvantage to such an arrangement is that you cannot limit the products covered to those approved by your broker-dealer. Some of the specialized Web site developers can offer customized product lists when you purchase their Web site development service.

CLIENT ACCOUNT ACCESS AND/OR CLIENT TRADING

ONE OF THE BIGGEST DRAWS you can provide on your site is client account access. Unfortunately, you do not have control over whether this option is offered. Most broker-dealers do offer this function. Nevertheless, not all offer it through a Web site link. Some broker-dealers allow access only through their corporate site.

Generally, client account access lets your clients see the status of their accounts (usually in real time) as well as some history—typically ninety days. Access is limited to brokerage accounts, because currently there is no way to consolidate nonbrokerage (direct) accounts. Account access can be a great time-saver for you since your clients no longer depend on you to answer routine questions regarding their accounts.

Client account trading is still relatively new within full-service brokerage houses. However, it is coming, because clients are demanding it. If you can't provide them this ability, at least a portion of their business will be done outside your view. This provides the opportunity for an online firm to pitch them other services. Unless you can convince them of your value, you will lose these clients eventually.

The research backs this up. A recent study by Cerulli Associates[2] indicates that online brokerages like Charles Schwab are moving upmarket. The percentage of customers having accounts with both a discount broker and a full-service firm grew from between 7 percent and 13 percent to between 15 percent and 30 percent. In fact, fully 34 percent of new customers for discount brokers were coming from full-service brokerages in 1999.

Ideally, you should provide this online trading capability seamlessly through your Web site, so that the client still identifies you as the provider of the online services. If you cannot do this yet, provide a link back to your broker-dealer's online trading site.

TERM QUOTES

TERM LIFE INSURANCE quote engines are available for use in rep Web sites or as stand-alone sites that you can link to. However, integrated quote engines have the advantage of not allowing a potential prospect or client to leave your site to get a quote. In addition, stand-alone quote sites cannot be tailored to your approved product list. Thus, a visitor could obtain a quote from a carrier that you are not contracted, licensed, or appointed to represent.

InsSite.net and Internet Pipeline Products' myagency.net develop insurance-oriented Web sites but also provide separate term quote engines that will integrate with your site (http://www.inssite.net/services.html or http://www.ipipeline.com/products/frame1e.htm).

MAP TO YOUR OFFICE

A SECTION THAT IS BECOMING increasingly popular is an interactive online map to your office. This allows the visitor to see your office location on a street map and to get driving directions from home. The first three services are free, and the last one requires software:

◆ **MapBlast** (http://www.mapblast.com/myblast/overview.mb?CMD=LFILL&IC=::8:&W=456&H=259)

◆ **MapQuest** (http://www.mapquest.com/cgi-bin/stat_parser?link=/b2b/b2b_homepage&uid=u9nu0gj2uchcydde:b2daysqz1)

◆ **Maps On Us** (http://mapsonus.com/doc/makemap.html)

◆ **ESRI** (http://www.esri.com). This has much more sophisticated mapping software and would be of the most use for larger offices with multiple locations.

ONLINE SURVEY

DEVELOPING AN ONLINE SURVEY is a way to keep people coming back to your site. The surveys can be but don't have to be serious; in fact, humorous or oddball surveys may be more attractive. Obviously, you can develop the content yourself, but Perseus Development Corporation (http://www.perseusdevelopment.com) can take the work out of it by helping with the online software and the survey design. The company even provides some simple free question and poll formats you can construct online and then download to your site.

REFER A FRIEND

A POPULAR FORM ALLOWS the visitor to enter referrals. It is interactive and allows the visitor to complete the fields online. It is then sent as an e-mail. See a sample of what this could look like at right.

CONTACT ME

DON'T FORGET THIS! This may sound silly, but in the rush of designing a site, with all its sexy new features, you can overlook this obvious but necessary feature. The Contact Me section can be either a simple e-mail link or a more complex form with pre-set fields that allow you to begin collecting data about the prospect or service information about a client. (It can even be more than one form.) How much and what information you collect depends in part on how you use your site in your marketing and service.

EVENTS CALENDAR

THIS IS AN ONLINE CALENDAR of your upcoming planned events or events you plan to participate in. The section is most useful if you hold regular seminars, which can be online seminars. You could also include finance-related community events, or if your site

Sample Referral Form

IF YOU FIND THIS SITE helpful and informative, please tell a friend. Much of our new business comes from referrals given to us by satisfied clients. Please take a couple of seconds to fill out this form. It is easy, and your friends will most likely appreciate the tip. Thank you for your support.

From: (your e-mail)
To: (your friend's e-mail)
Subject: "Great Financial Services Site"

(Your friend's name):
   I just found a great site for financial information. I find it very useful, and I thought you might as well.
                    http://www.yoursite.com
Check it out, and let me know what you think!

(Your name)

is targeted toward a particular demographic, include events they would be interested in attending.

NEWSLETTERS AND ARTICLES

NEWSLETTERS AND ARTICLES can be powerful tools on a Web site if they are topical and hold the reader's interest. They can add to the credibility of the representative by highlighting his professionalism, training, and experience. Even if the rep is not the author, a good topical article can reflect well on the rep. It's the "Gee, this guy is really on top of things!" effect. It's easy to integrate online content and use it to complement other forms of marketing (i.e., "See my latest newsletter on www.repsite.com for more on this topic").

You have several choices here. You can create new content. To do this, you will have to do some research on industry trends or product information. A list of good article research sites is included in Appendix B. Some site developers offer a newsletter template as part of their development services. This will allow you to write and post your newsletter online. In some instances, you can post these newsletters well in advance of when they automatically appear on your site.

You can also find vendors that will provide content that you can use in your newsletter or in other places on your site. For example, Morningstar's Quicktakes Plus program allows you, for a fee, to choose what content you want from the information on its site (http://www.morningstar.com/products/coqp.html). Both AdvisorSites (http://www.advisorsites.com/advisorsites/f_content.html) and Web Dynamics (http://www.myfrontdoor.com/tools.html) offer a range of in-depth NASD-reviewed content you can integrate with an existing site.

The Financial Planning Consultants site (www.financialsoftware.com) offers a text library system containing sample documents and ready-to-publish articles for financial advisers. Financial Visions (http://financialvisions.com/html/financial.htp) also offers free stand-alone content for your site. Many of the vendors that provide specialized financial service Web sites also offer online newsletters or articles as part of their Web site package.

Writing a newsletter requires a considerable commitment of time. You may wonder how you will ever be able to maintain your newsletter and keep current articles on your site. One way is to hire a freelance writer or a ghostwriter. Wealth Writers (www.wealthwriters.com) specializes in financial service client articles and client newsletters. The Newsletter Factory offers newsletter templates, enabling you to develop your own, and a stable of writers who can provide content for you (www.newsletterfactory.ca).

There are also a number of bulletin-board sites for writers where you can post your topic request. Here are several examples.

◆ **Authorlink** (http://www.authorlink.com)
◆ **The Writer's Exchange at About.com** (http://writerexchange.about.com/arts/writerexchange/?once=true&)
◆ **The Writer's Place** (http://www.awoc.com/AWOC-Home.cfm)
◆ **Writer's Resource Center** (http://www.poewar.com)

In addition, a staff placement agency exists that focuses on writers. It offers both temporary and permanent employment (http://www.staffwriters.com/index.cfm).

The other main option would be to use a newsletter designed for use with financial service clients. Unfortunately, the major players in this market have not yet repackaged or repriced their products for online use. Keep close tabs on this, since it is inevitable that someone will offer this type of service. Some of the key players include the American Society of CLU & ChFC, Emerald Publications, Financial Literacy Center, First Marketing Company, Integrated Concepts Group, and Liberty Publications. The Andy Gluck Newsletters are part of the AdvisorSites group, and while the newsletters are not yet available, some specially designed content (as mentioned above) is available.

LAYOUT, PHOTOS, AND GRAPHICS

AT FIRST GLANCE, you may be wondering why I've even included this section. It is true that much of the layout, photos, and graphics for a template site are for the most part outside your control. Even with custom site developers, you are counting on their expertise in the use of these elements—that's why you hired them in the first place.

Well, there are several good reasons to understand the basic concepts of layout, photos, and graphics. First, you do need to understand the impact of these elements so that you can properly evaluate a template site developer's work. Second, when you develop a custom site, the designer has a much better chance of developing something that meets your needs if you can speak the language. Third, from time to time, you will be contributing photos or graphic elements. You need to know the rules so you send the proper file size and best file format to your developer.

Besides the basic do's and don'ts discussed earlier, let's look at some tips for keeping your site sharp-looking but efficient.

◆ **Visitor's view.** Most visitors view Web sites at 800 by 600 resolution on their fifteen-inch monitors. Your site must be designed so that all your navigation and key headlines appear on the monitor's screen at that resolution. Don't make your visitors scroll out or down in order to read necessary navigation or key points. This may be the first contact you'll have with a potential prospect! The visitor needs to be able to immediately recognize and use your site.

◆ **Graphics and load time.** You need to be aware of several design limitations inherent to the Web. Photos, colors, or graphics that look great in print may look odd when they appear on a monitor. Graphics that work well in a layout may take two or three minutes to load into a visitor's browser.

You need to design your graphics specifically for the Web. To do this, you need to create the best blend of quality and speed when presenting your site. Remember that load time is critical to the success of a Web site. It ranks on a par with the content of the site. It doesn't matter what you have to say on your site if there is no one there to read it! Make sure that your site is quick to load, no matter what you put on it.

Avoid excessively large photo or graphic files. The height and width of an image, as measured in pixels,[3] is called the resolution. Resolution of graphics and images for your Web pages should be no more than 72 dpi. The smaller the files' size, the better.

Although faster connection speeds are now available, most visitors to your site will be dialing in at 28.8 kilobytes per second. In actual throughput, these users are getting about 1 kilobyte per second under very favorable conditions, and 200 bytes or fewer per second when the connections are slogged with traffic. This is a very narrow nozzle through which to push your graphics and photos.

A small, 30K file takes thirty seconds to load at best and two-and-a-half minutes when being accessed under heavy traffic. That's longer than most people willingly wait. To be successful, a page should load completely in twenty seconds or less. To keep the reader's attention, it is a good idea to keep images less than 25 kilobytes, with an optimal range of 12 to 15. (As a rule of thumb, your entire main page should be about 50K. If you have significantly more information to impart than can be contained in these file sizes, split your content and add more pages.)

Another trick to convince impatient Web surfers to wait is to let them see something happening. You can add the feeling of more speed by having your designer save JPEG files with the "progressive attribute" or GIF files as "interlaced." In most browsers, these attributes will make the images appear all at once, then sharpen gradually.

◆ **GIF versus JPEG.** The Web demands trade-offs between quality and size. The most commonly used image file types you'll see on Web sites today are ".gif" and ".jpg," known as GIFs (CompuServe Graphic Interchange Format) and JPEGs (Joint Photographic Experts Group). Choosing the correct file format for the images and artwork on your pages is very important. Use GIFs for line art, drawings, and solid colors, or for any graphics you create in your paint or image-editing programs. GIFs use eight-bit color (only 256 colors), so they are ideal for images with a small color range. Small Web graphics saved in GIF format should not exceed 10 kilobytes. However, GIFs are not good for photographs, because a photo has a large color range.

Photographs and elements with blends and graduations look best when saved as JPEGs. JPEGs use twenty-four-bit color (millions of colors). The JPEG format uses a type of compression that results in a trade-off between file size and quality. In general, a JPEG's larger color range will make photographs look much better on your Web page, while a GIF looks much better with solid colors.

◆ **Keeping your graphics cost down.** If you can provide Web-ready graphics on disk, in either the GIF or JPEG formats, you can hold your development cost down. If a Web site vendor has to develop new graphics and artwork or scan them in, it will add to your cost, and the resulting files may not be useful for other media. Tip: Develop both a high-resolution (for print) and an Internet-resolution version of your company's identity files so that you can use them consistently in all of your marketing.

◆ **Where to go for help.** If you need help in getting your logo digitized or your photo scanned, look in the yellow pages for prepress shops, printers, or graphic designers. These shops can usually provide the experience and quality of output needed for both high-resolution printing and low-resolution Web site graphics. However, ask specifically about their experience in preparing files for use with the Internet. If experienced, these shops will be able to repurpose the files to lower resolutions for use with your Web site.

To obtain online graphics you can access online libraries like Icons and Stuff (http://www.xs4all.nl/~arjenvm/pics/index.

html). This index of online resources allows downloading of elements like bullets, icons, and ruler bars. Bullets come in all sizes, shapes, and colors, and are easily available. Icons, such as the "caution" sign for pages under construction or standard icons for file folders, sound files, and so on, are also available. Ruler bars, which come in various lengths, widths, and colors, can be used to separate sections of the page. Remember, too, that if you are attempting to match something already on your site, you can also ask your developers to send you the graphics file they used via the Internet.

There are many stock photo and graphic companies available on the Internet. From them you can choose images and graphics to use on your high-resolution pieces as well as your Web site. Examples of pay image sites are PhotoDisc (http://www.photodisc. com) and EyeWire (http://www.imageclub.com).

More information about design and desktop publishing resources can be found at sites like desktopPublishing.com (http://www.desktoppublishing.com) and About.com's Graphic Design section (http://graphicdesign.miningco.com/arts/graphic design/).

◆ **Check out your site.** If you are having a custom site developed, check your layout, graphics, colors, and backgrounds by having some people log on to your site while it is still in development. These testers should not be from within the industry and should be representative of the type of clients you wish to attract. You, your developer, or your Web site host should be able to provide these testers with special access; remember, your site is not yet visible to the entire Internet community. Be sure they log on at 28 kilobytes per second from a computer using 800 by 600 resolution and a fifteen-inch monitor. Many times, a couple of opinions can lead to useful changes in design direction.

◆ **Links to other sites.** Be very cautious in providing links from your site to other sites. Keep in mind that each link is like an exit from your site. Once visitors leave by that doorway, you may never get them back again! Any link you provide should be in some way related to the purpose of your site. Unrelated links simply distract visitors from why they went to your site in the first place. Your compliance department should review all the sites you plan to provide links to. And remind visitors that they are leaving your site when they click on an external link. Remember, you don't want to be held accountable for any information provided on those sites—be sure you have a disclaimer on your site to that effect.

Building Specialized Niche Sites

WHAT I'VE JUST DESCRIBED are the contents of a *typical* rep Web site. This certainly does not exhaust the possible contents of rep Web sites. You may find that the traditional rep Web site doesn't fit the type of marketing that you do. In this case, you need to develop a more specialized site. As a rule, such sites are nearly always designed by a custom site developer. These sites are much more targeted. They tend to focus on how you market, what you market, or to whom you market—in other words, a niche market.

It is also worth noting that the traditional site and the specialized niche site are not mutually exclusive. You may find that you need both types to support your business. The specialized site may provide you with the focused support for a particular marketing effort, while the traditional site provides the broader service and ongoing support your clients need for the rest of their portfolio. You may even find that you need more than one specialized site. Several examples of specialized sites were discussed in Chapters 2, 3, and 4. More information and some additional examples follow.

SEMINAR/CONFERENCE SITES

IF YOUR PRIMARY METHOD of marketing is seminars, then it might make sense to have a seminar site. Rather than giving a broad overview of the rep's services, as the conventional site does, a seminar site focuses on the promotion and presentation of seminars. It provides supplementary support (registration, downloadable materials, schedules, dates, times, places, agendas, outlines, etc.) as well as possibly hosting the seminar itself. A seminar can be broadcast live or delayed. That option allows you to reach a much broader audience and can eliminate many of the excuses prospects give for not attending. An online seminar also offers the advantage of being much less threatening to the prospect than attendance at a live seminar.

If you want to host the seminar online, you can be as simple or as complex as you want. At the simple end of the scale is breaking your seminar apart and placing it on separate HTML Web pages with GIF or JPEG files for charts and other visuals. This is quick and cheap—in addition, unless you add too many graphics, it loads quickly. However, if your seminar is of any length, you may find that this approach quickly becomes boring for your visitor.

The next step is an online slide show. This can be designed with a presentation program like Microsoft PowerPoint and easily placed online. This approach is visually more interesting but takes longer to load. The same thing can be accomplished using online applications like Macromedia's Shockwave, though it is not as intuitive to set up.

Another option is to use either specialized software or the support of a company that provides online hosting. As mentioned in the section on "Online Sales Seminars" in Chapter 5, a number of vendors specialize in providing online support for live or delayed Webcasts:

◆ **Astound** (http://www.astound.com): Sales and hosting

◆ **Cisco Systems' Cisco Seminars and Events Online** (http://webevents.broadcast.com/cisco/ciscolive/home.asp): Sales only—high-end system for large meetings

◆ **Epiphany's iMeet** (http://imeet.com): Hosting only—free use for fewer than five users and less than sixty minutes; simple system best for smaller meetings

◆ **Evoke Communications** (http://www.evoke.com): Sales and hosting—sophisticated system; excellent for large seminar use

◆ **Microsoft's NetMeeting** (http://www.microsoft.com/windows/netmeeting/?RLD=52): Sales only—simple system, best for smaller meetings

◆ **PlaceWare** (http://www.placeware.com): Sales—sophisticated system, excellent for large seminar use. ASP hosting—platform is available at a lower one-time-event cost. Full meeting support and services are available, including marketing, reminders, billing, etc.

◆ **Seminar Source.com** (http://www.seminarsource.com): Same as above.

◆ **WebEx.com** (http://www.webex.com/): Same as above.

One seminar approach is to use a live online slide show pulled directly off the presenter's computer with either Internet- or phone-based audio. The presentation can be either a simultaneous broadcast from a live seminar or a stand-alone Internet broadcast. With the live presentation, still photos can be shown of the seminar and audience. The participants can interact with the speaker in real time, and they can go to a chat room to interact with each other. In addition, a virtual seating chart is assigned as part of the online registration process. This approach is about as sophisticated as you can get without running into bandwidth problems with the general-public participants. As it is, those with 28K modems will experience some delays in graphics displays and breaks in the Internet-based audio, although audio problems can be avoided by using the phone for audio.

Moving up another step would be to Webcast your seminars with streaming video and audio. This presents significant bandwidth problems and is considerably more expensive. However, if your audience is sufficiently upscale or primarily businesses, this may be an excellent option. The premier firm for this type of service is Akamai (http://www.akamai.com).

No matter what approach you use, you'll need to have a registration process, even if you don't charge for your seminar, in order to capture information about your prospects so you can follow up. When a third party is providing the registration, you will need to review the sign-up form to be sure it obtains the correct information.

If you do plan to charge for your seminar (or any other product or service on your site), you may need to have an e-commerce capability built into your site. While you can handle Internet transactions offline, increasingly visitors expect to be able to do their business online. Some of the ASPs are developing this capability, but there are a number of firms that specialize in such services. For additional e-commerce information, visit Wilson Internet E-commerce Resources (http://www.wilsonweb.com/commerce). Some of the Webcasting providers mentioned earlier either have or are developing an e-commerce component.

Note: If you use a third-party provider's content for your seminar, you will need to discuss with them whether there are any special restrictions regarding the use of their material as part of an online presentation. There are a number of such providers; two of the largest include

◆ **Successful Money Management Seminars** (http://sales. smms.com)

◆ **Emerald Publications** (http://emeraldpublications.com/sems/ seminars.htm)

Here are some examples from various industries of what online seminar sites might look like. These sites are not intended as examples of how to build a great site but only to show the types of online seminar experiences currently available.

◆ **The Bank of Montreal Online Seminar Series** (http://www. on-lineseminars.com). This is a combination of a slide show with audio clips.

◆ **ePlanning.com** (http://www.eplanning.com) is a planning firm specializing in seminars. Its approach combines a chat room, live seminars, and online training.

◆ **Manufacturing Systems** (http://webevents.broadcast.com/ manufacturingsystems/broadcast041200/home.asp). The company has purchased software to fully support online seminars, similar to what PlaceWare offers. Options exist to listen live via two different audio players and to view the presentation. You also have the option to download the presentation.

MARKET-SPECIFIC NICHE SITES

NICHE MARKET SITES are designed to support a particular product or service. The areas of specialization are endless, from small business to estate to college to pension. This kind of specialized niche site is a relatively recent development, but the opportunities are certainly available. If you have developed a market niche, have extensive experience with a particular product or program, or have a unique marketing approach, you may want to consider developing a program site.

These sites are always built from the perspective of the potential customer. You need to write down those things that make your services valuable to your customers. Be very specific. Think in terms of the products, services, and support you offer. What about those things will appeal to your clients? Call some of your clients and ask them. Then think about which of those products and services could be moved online. What could you offer more efficiently or effectively online? Be creative! Think big! Don't assume that something can't be done online simply because you haven't heard of it being accomplished that way.

To be successful, the site must be core to your marketing efforts. Think about how it could become central to your marketing. There has to be a compelling reason for a visitor to come to your site in the first place and to return in the future. As a rule, this type of site is more successful if it is professionally developed (see the section on "Ownership Issues" in Chapter 7). These sites must have a very professional look and feel.

Vendors are also beginning to provide specialized online support services to reps who specialize in certain highly targeted markets. An example is LifeGoals Corporation's LGM Online™, a site that provides support to financial advisers who are recommending mortgage strategies to improve their clients' financial situations (http://www.lifegoals.com/internet/onlinemort/default.asp).

PROSPECT-SPECIFIC NICHE SITES

IF YOU MARKET TO A SPECIFIC demographic or ethnic community, a prospect-specific site may be a good option for you. Sites that focus on women, retired people, African-Americans, etc., can be very effective if constructed properly and with respect for the needs and traditions of that group. There is also a wealth of content material available as well as links to other sites focused on that same community.

You should use the same process described in "Prospect-Specific Niche Sites" to develop your site. However, these sites can also encompass services that are specific to the demographic or ethnic group being served. These services should be a result of your clients' input. As with any niche site, this type of Web site needs to be core to your marketing to be successful.

How Good Is Your Site?

"HEY! I ALREADY HAVE A SITE—what about me?" That's great—you're ahead of most adviser offices. Nevertheless, the important point isn't to have a site (that's the easy part) but to have a *good* site. So how do you tell? A hint: If you haven't revised your site's content in a month—even if your site has won awards—you have a bad site!

As I've mentioned earlier, one way to evaluate your site is to look at both good and bad examples of sites and compare. If you haven't already done so, look at the award-winning sites selected by the review sites listed in the "Finding Good Sites" section in Chapter 6. Look at the features your site and these sites have in common. Look for good ideas you might be able to adapt. Make some notes so you can use them later when you revise your site.

There are also several sites that specialize in evaluating Web sites and giving you constructive criticism (some for a fee and some for free). Having someone give you an objective opinion can be very helpful:

◆ **Critics Corner** (http://www.critics-corner.com)
◆ **My Site Stinks** (http://www.mysitestinks.com/index.htm)
◆ **Siegel Vision** (http://www.siegelvision.com)
◆ **WebInspect** (http://www.webinspect.com)

Finally, go to the best source of all: Ask your clients. What do they like? What do they not like? Can they find what they are looking for on your site? If not, find out why. There may come a time when a template site is simply too structured to meet the specific needs of your clients, and you may need to look at spending a bit more money and developing a custom site. This kind of evaluation is the best way to find out if you're at that point.

How often do clients visit your site? You should have some statistics to help you here. Whoever is hosting your site should be able to give you a printout of your traffic for the last few months. If your clients visit once and don't return, you have problems. (Again, be sure you are measuring "visits" and not "hits.")

This client site evaluation should be done regularly—every three to six months. You can mail it as a postcard or letter or do it over the phone. Schedule it like any other client contact. After all, it gives you one more nonthreatening reason to call them. Establish a set of questions that will give you good information (see the survey below).

Caution: Be realistic on your expectations regarding the number of prospects and clients that visit your site each month. Remember that it is much less important how many visits, than it is that they came away favorably impressed.

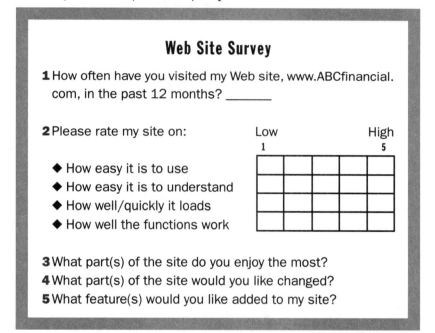

Web Site Survey

1 How often have you visited my Web site, www.ABCfinancial. com, in the past 12 months? _____

2 Please rate my site on:

	Low 1				High 5
How easy it is to use					
How easy it is to understand					
How well/quickly it loads					
How well the functions work					

3 What part(s) of the site do you enjoy the most?
4 What part(s) of the site would you like changed?
5 What feature(s) would you like added to my site?

7

WEB SITE DEVELOPERS

IT SEEMS THAT EVERYONE TODAY is a Web site developer. Nearly every Internet service provider (ISP) provides Web development services. Most advertising agencies provide Web development. There are thousands of independent Web design services available. Specialized firms develop sites for specific types of industries. Consulting firms offer to create your entire Web site strategy—and "Oh, by the way, we also develop Web sites." How do you choose? What makes a good Web developer?

Finding a Developer

ONE OF THE THINGS you'll discover in interviewing potential developers is that all developers are not created equal. Find out where their skills lie. At a minimum, any developer you hire must be able to code Web pages and understand how to promote your site online (see Chapter 8, "Marketing and Promoting Your Web Site"). Unless you plan to use clip art, stock photos, or stock graphics, they'll need to be capable of doing original graphic artwork (ask for some samples). Make sure they have experience in developing the kinds of features you want on your site (such as e-mail forms, search engines, discussion boards, guest books, chat rooms, etc.).[1]

If you plan to use an industry-specialist developer (either template or custom), your review process is a bit easier, since you can actually look at sites they have developed for firms similar to yours. You can also go to their user sites and ask the users if they are satisfied. Since the user is in the same basic market selling the same basic services as you, it is relatively easy to screen them.

However, if you plan to use a generalist developer, you need to do more homework. It is hard to evaluate an excellent educational site or an excellent automotive-parts site and determine whether this developer can build an excellent financial services site. One of the better places to find unbiased information on Web developers is CNET.com's Web services section under Web Developers (http://webservices.cnet.com/html/aisles/Web_Developers.asp). Here you can view side-by-side comparisons of developers. You can even screen your potential candidates by their skill sets. The major drawbacks are that this is a very small list (about thirty-five firms). Also, most of these developers are larger firms and thus will generally be more costly. Two larger directories that also provide some level of basic screening are eConstructors (http://www.econstructors. com/buy/binfo/.html) and elance (http://www.elance.com/ c/cats/main/categories.pl?catId=10183&rid=66NM). Both firms have the advantage of allowing the developers to bid for your business online.

There is likely to be some very good local talent in your area that does not appear on any of these lists. There are some definite advantages to using local developers. Developing a site long-distance, while feasible, is more time-consuming and potentially more costly than using local Web developers if not managed carefully.

The bottom line, though, is that for most generalist developers, the best method (especially for the local ones) is to ask other businesses for referrals. Obviously, finding a developer that has some experience developing a site for a financial service rep is best. However, this is a very small segment of the sites being developed— so don't count on this. Look instead for referrals from true commercial sites (nonprofit, educational, governmental, or private sites do not require the same approach as a commercial site). Look also for sites that deal with the public (not business-to-business). The closer the reference's site is to the type of marketing and services you intend to provide for your customers, the better.

Once you contact a potential developer, be sure to ask for additional references from other customers. Once you get a referral, you need to ask the referring business some very specific questions about the quality of the developer's work. Here are some good questions to ask:

◆ **How long has the site been operational?** You want to avoid situations in which the site has only been up for a few months. First, there are always initial glitches when a site goes up. Second, there is no real way to tell how successful a site has been if there is no track record.

◆ **Did the developer do a good job in a timely manner?** Find out if the developer proposed innovations to the design or merely did what the customer instructed. You are hiring, in part, their design expertise, so you should get your money's worth. Find out the site's original proposed delivery date. By how much did that date slip? Unless the site in question is extraordinarily complex, a delay of more than two months should be a red flag. Find out if they offer any delivery date guarantees.

◆ **Is the Web site accomplishing its marketing goals?** No matter how great the site looks, if it is not accomplishing the purpose for which it was built, it is a failure. Ask questions like "What percentage of your business now comes to you as a result of your site?" or "What percentage of your client service is now handled online as a result of this site?"

◆ **Were there any hidden or unexpected costs?**

◆ **How have your customers received the site?** Don't be satisfied with "well." Ask for specific comments about features customers like or dislike.

Look at the reference's site. Try out the features and functions. Some features may be password-protected, so ask the reference for a temporary password so you can test it. You should also look at other examples of the same developer's work.

Does Your Developer Understand Marketing?

IF YOU ARE EXPECTING your developer to market your site for you, you will be disappointed. That responsibility, just like any other form of marketing your practice, is yours. A developer's primary responsibility is to assist you in designing, building, and maintaining your site. However, any good developer should provide the marketing basics. Your developer should be able to tell you

◆ How to write content for your Web site to make it appealing to your Web audience

◆ How search engines work and how your Web site should be designed to optimize your site's search results

◆ How to register your Web site with the major search engines and directories

◆ The value of exchanging links with other Web sites

◆ Other methods of marketing that are appropriate for your Web site (don't, however, expect the developer to implement these for you)

This is only the starting place and is not nearly sufficient to integrate your Web site into your overall marketing efforts. Don't expect the developer to understand your industry (unless she's a specialist developer). However, if the answers you are getting to the above questions leave you feeling uncomfortable with the individual's understanding of general Web site marketing, look elsewhere!

Ownership Issues

BEFORE HIRING A DEVELOPER, it is important to establish who will hold copyright over your Web site's design, content, and graphics. Some developers insist that they retain copyright. This means that should you discontinue use of the developer's services, the developer gets to keep your Web site! In addition, you won't be able to have another company alter your Web site. Insist that you be given copyright over the Web site's design, content, and graphics and that a copyright notice to that effect is placed some-where on your Web site.

There are a number of exceptions to this rule. The first is pro-grams used to run Web site features like discussion boards, chat rooms, guest books, virtual cards, etc. Often it is not possible to obtain the rights to the program code, or if you do, it's expensive. Usually, you will obtain a license to use the code on your Web site, or you may just rent the service the program provides.

The second exception is template sites. A template site is one that provides standardized features and layouts that you can cus-tomize (within limits) to meet your particular needs. This type of site is usually cheaper since it requires less custom work by the developer. If a general developer is working on your site, you should avoid template sites because of the aforementioned copy-right problems.

However, this may not be true if a financial services industry spe-cialist is working on a template site for you. Many of the features and functions designed into such an industry-specific template site are very costly to duplicate on a stand-alone basis. In some instances, these features are custom designed, copyrighted, and available only as part of the template. However, you need to under-stand up front that a template site developer will retain the copy-right to the template components on his site. Thus, you do not have the ability to decide to move your site to a new hosting firm or to host it yourself. You also cannot modify any portion of the tem-plate, even to fully integrate new functions or features into it. If you require this kind of flexibility, you need to use a custom site devel-oper. (See "Specialists" below for more discussion on templates.)

Hosting

THE TERM *HOSTING* REFERS TO the physical location—the actual computer—where your Web site program actually resides. Many developers also offer hosting and have packages that include both hosting and developing at a discounted price. You don't have to host with the developer, and in some cases it may be to your advan-tage not to, particularly if you intend to do the hosting yourself at some point. However, I don't recommend this unless you have a very large office and very robust computer system. In any case, if you plan to use a template site developer, you don't have a choice: you must host with the developer.

CNET.com's Web services section contains an excellent segment on Web hosting (http://webservices.cnet.com/html/aisles/ Web_Hosting.asp) that discusses the various hosting options and provides screens to look at various vendors' offerings. A number of sites also rank or rate Web hosting services:

◆ **Host Compare** (http://www.hostcompare.com/comparisons. htm)

◆ **ISPcheck** (http://ispcheck.com)

◆ **The US ISP Ratings** (http://www.inversenet.com/products/ ims/ratings)

◆ **TopHosts.com** (http://www.tophosts.com/pages/topover 01.htm)

◆ **Web Host Directory, Web Host Awards** (http://webhostdir.com/ webhostawards)

Note that many of these services also do a general rating on the Internet service provider's other services, so even if you are not planning to host a Web site, these sites are a good source of information on the reliability of your ISP.

Generalists

GENERALIST DEVELOPERS create sites for a wide range of businesses. There is nothing wrong with this type of developer. Many do excellent work. However, unique constraints apply to the insurance, securities, and investment advisory industries. These developers are unlikely to be aware of these constraints. State licensing regulations, NASD requirements, and SEC rulings make the wording and even the graphics displayed on a site subject to compliance regulation.

You, the developer, and your compliance department will need to work closely if you are to avoid costly revisions and delays in making your site operational. You need to make your developer aware up front of the compliance review delays that are built into the site approval process. They can then consider this in their development quote. You also need to discuss with them the compliance procedures for updating your site; don't assume they understand. If you are not careful, compliance changes can significantly hold up the development or revision of your site and may affect the cost, since you may be charged if you have an unusual number of revisions.

Further, many specialist developers in financial service sites have automated the compliance approval component of the initial and subsequent revision process. This means your site can be approved and edited much faster than with the manual process you will be forced to use with a generalist developer. A generalist developer is also unlikely to have many of the industry-specific functions already built, which would be an additional cost and time factor for you.

Look at your Web site goals and marketing plan to see if a generalist developer can meet your needs at a reasonable cost. The more industry-specific functions you need on your site, the less likely a generalist developer will be the right choice for you.

Specialists

A NUMBER OF WEB SITE DEVELOPERS specialize in sites for the financial services industry. These specialists offer some distinct advantages. First, they are familiar with the industry, how to market your site, and how to deal with the compliance procedures you must deal with. Second, many of the calculators, online planning functions, data feeds, product information links, and broker-dealer integration functions have already been addressed or built.

Specialist developers generally offer either template sites or custom sites, although a few offer both.

TEMPLATE SITES

A TEMPLATE SITE IS database-driven, and while considerable variation is allowed, all sites are built using a template with the same basic structure. To create your site you go through an online "back-office" site. This site allows you to select the look of your site from a menu of designs and color schemes. You add your personal information, articles, newsletters, and other content online through this same site. You also select the optional interactive functions you wish to have appear. Updates are handled the same way. This back-office site allows you to easily keep your content fresh. All template sites are hosted on a central server; thus, you must host your site with the developer.

In some instances, these template sites are "sponsored" by a broker-dealer or carrier. Along with much lower pricing, this allows the site to be customized to the needs of a particular sponsor. This may mean access to broker-dealer-specific functions like client account access. Usually a compliance engine integrates with the online back-office function of the sponsored site so that the site review and approval process can be automated. This setup allows easier and faster updates to the site.

The template site approach has some limitations. First, the developer does not have the flexibility to support specialized niche sites. Such sites require content and functions that are not available on a template site. This means that if you plan to use your site for things like online seminars or highly targeted market niches, the template site is a poor choice.

Second, template site designs are owned and hosted by the developer. Thus, if you decide to later move your site, you will need to redesign it from scratch, and you will not be able to use many of the features on your existing site since the developer holds the copyrights. Third, template sites do not handle large offices with multiple locations particularly well. Although it is possible to use a template site with a large office, it may be cumbersome to administer and potentially more costly than a custom site.

CUSTOMIZED SITES

CUSTOMIZED SITES ALLOW the developer to lay out and program each page to your specifications and thus offer much more control of the design of your site. Currently there are very few truly specialized custom financial services site developers, though there are some generalist developers with experience developing rep sites. Custom developers may also be sponsored (or partially sponsored) by a broker-dealer or carrier, and these developers may or may not provide back-office or compliance engine functions.

Here are some examples of financial service site specialist developers offering either template or custom sites for securities and/or insurance specialties:

◆ **ADVISORport.com** (http://advisorport.com). Offered only as a part of an online client and office management system

◆ **AdvisorSites** (http://www.advisorsites.com/advisorsites/index .html). Template and custom sites

◆ **AdvisorSquare** (http://www.advisorsquare.com/advisorsquare/ intro)

◆ **Amicus, Inc.** (http://www.amicus.com/gateway/cgi?k=guest login2). Available only through contracted broker-dealers or carriers and not directly to representatives

◆ **ChannelNet Internet Group.** New to the United States; principal experience with British financial adviser sites; owned by the Soft-Ad Group, a fifteen-year-old software company with offices in London, Detroit, Chicago, and San Francisco (see http://www.assure web.co.uk for an example)

◆ **Emerald Web Sites** (http://www.emeraldWeb sites.com/Web sites/Web sites.htm)

◆ **Financial Profiles' Profiles Online** (http://financialprofiles. com/products/advisor-Web sites/default.asp)

◆ **Financial Visions Web Sites** (http://www.focusonplanning.com)

◆ **Info-One** (http://www.info-one.com). Offers insurance and securities-oriented custom sites for larger offices

◆ **InsSite.net** (http://www.inssite.net/services.html)

◆ **LifeGoals' LGWeb** (http://www.lifegoals.com)

◆ **Lightport.com** (http://home2.lightport.com)

◆ **RIAnet** (http://www.rianet.com/websites.html). Offers securities template Web sites for the Registered Investment Advisor

◆ **WebAgencies.com** (http://www.webagencies.com). Offers insurance-oriented template Web sites, including property/casualty

◆ **Web Dynamics** (http://www.myfrontdoor.com)

MARKETING
AND
PROMOTING
YOUR
WEB SITE

OK, How Do They Find Me?

NO SITE WILL MAKE a sale for you. No site will service your clients for you. Sites don't sell, and sites don't service—you do! No matter how sophisticated your site is, you will never be able to flip a switch, put your feet up, and forget about it. Developing a good Web site takes time and effort, on both an initial and an ongoing basis. This is true even when you are having a professional develop the site for you.

While you shouldn't try to become a Web developer, you can't simply hand over your Web site marketing to a professional developer and walk away. Most developers (even those with substantial experience working in financial services) are not great marketers. They know how to build a great-looking and -functioning site. They cannot integrate it into your overall marketing plan—only you can do that. Using your Web site to market or service takes just as much work as any other method of sales and service—it's just different.

Developing a Site Concept

SOME BASIC STEPS are involved in creating a good Web site. Let's touch on each one first, and then go into more detail on the specifics later.

◆ **Determine your goal.** Ask yourself what you want to do with your site. Look at your Internet marketing plan. Then consider your strategy for the site. Do you want to service existing clients from your site? Do you want to sell using your site? Do you want your site to focus on only one or two key products or services that you want to promote, explain, or use for consumer education? Do you want to have an entertaining and fun site that will make the user keep coming back? Do you want an all-encompassing site where the user can find whatever he needs? Do you want a very simple site with only the basic information clients need to contact you? Do you want your clients to do things on your site without involving you (client account lookup, online interactive forms, trading, etc.)?

Be specific in your answers. List all the reasons. Write down your answers. Set them aside and look at them again after a few days. Do they still make sense?

If they do, create a demographic for your Web site. Reread your Internet marketing plan to refresh your memory on who your target audience is going to be. Now, create a realistic two- or three-sentence goal for your Web site.

◆ **Lay out your Web site.** Before you do anything, you need to get a picture in your mind of what your site will look like when you're done. Will you have a lot of Web pages or just a few? How many graphics do you want? Do you want animation, sound, or video? Write your thoughts down on a piece of paper, or better yet, draw a basic diagram (see the sample Web diagram).

Note that at this point, the design is pretty general. You are really interested not in how the site looks but in how it works. This will help you figure out what you need on your site. I'll discuss template

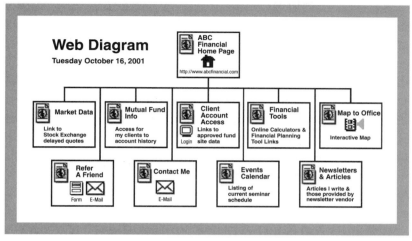

site development in more detail later, but this step and the next are very important in evaluating whether a template site will work for you or whether you need a custom-designed site. Keep your overall layout in mind while you're doing the other steps.

◆ **Develop a storyboard.** This doesn't mean you need to draw little pictures of what each page will look like. Instead, try to write down what each page will contain and the information you will try to convey. This storyboard becomes very important when you evaluate template sites or solicit site development bids.

◆ **Find some examples of sites you like.** Look for sites that have both a purpose similar to yours and a look and feel you like. Look at how they organized their information or links. Note how they designed their pages. Make notes as you go and/or print those pages you like. Then go back and modify your storyboard and site structure.

◆ **Look for links.** While you're researching, look for places to which you could link. These sites can include more information on a topic you discuss, or they can be regulatory or governmental sites. However, be selective. Each linked site must contribute to the overall goal of your site. Cut and paste the URL and title of the Web site onto a page in your word processor and then add the reason why you liked the site. Later, you can create (or have created) a link or a links page from within your site. Keep in mind, however, that all of these links will need to be reviewed by your compliance department. Also, remember that all links carry a danger that your site visitor will leave your site, never to return.

◆ **Create your Web site.** Here you have several choices. You can have a site built for you. Plenty of firms will design and build your site, and some will offer to host it, too. However, since site developers charge for edits, it makes sense (and is less costly to you) to choose one that is already familiar with adviser Web site development. Because your compliance department must give final approval before your site goes live, you need to be sure your site is not accessible by the public while it is under development (do not assume this is the case, particularly with developers that have little experience with our market).

Developers with experience in our industry offer both template sites or custom sites. In some cases, your broker-dealer may already provide a representative Web site program. Since the broker-dealer can negotiate with a site developer on behalf of a large number of representatives, these are usually less costly than those developed individually.

◆ **Have a beta test.** Never go live with your site before you have had a chance to test it! Most developers build a test period into their development timeline; make sure you ask them about it. Ask your friends to check out your Web site, and have them tell you what they thought. Ask them how fast it loaded, if it looked OK, if they would come back again. Try to incorporate their comments into your Web site. Check your site with more than one browser to help you make it more compatible with other browsers.

◆ **Review and update regularly.** Keep your Web site up-to-date. Make content changes at least monthly. Plan to revise the site's design annually. If you have a template site, check with your developer to find out when new templates or features will be added. Static sites do not get return traffic. Be on the lookout for anything that might interest your prospects or clients. Even template sites can add links to additional content or functions, in many cases seamlessly adding these changes to your existing site. If this content comes from outside vendors, check with your compliance department first.

Look for ways to build traffic to your site. Where can you add links from other sites? How can you integrate your site into your other marketing? How can you make it easier for visitors to find your site? Periodically, reanalyze your Web site. Is it still consistent with your marketing strategy? Has your strategy changed? Start the process all over again and upgrade your Web site or, if necessary, change vendors.

Promoting Your Web Site

ACTUALLY, YOUR FIRST QUESTION should be "What am I going to use this site for?" If your site is used primarily as a client service vehicle, then promoting your site to the general public is a wasted effort (there are other techniques to drive clients to your site). However, if your site's purpose is to attract new business, then you need to make sure your prospects can find you. This section will help you help your developer enhance your site's visibility to search engines and directories. Certain things make your site attractive and others make it unattractive (some will even turn your site into a pariah).

◆ **It is important that you take the time to understand the impact that certain design, layout, and marketing approaches have on your site's accessibility to prospects.** This is true even when you are having your site built by a professional developer. Remember, a developer's principal job and area of expertise is making your site attractive and user-friendly. The majority of developers do not concern themselves with the search-engine-visibility aspect of site design. *Never assume your developer has designed your site for maximum visibility.* Even with a template site, with which you have little control over site design, your developer or an Internet marketing specialist can better direct search engines to your site by adding "doorway pages" or using other techniques discussed below.

In addition, as a site owner, numerous marketing companies will offer to enhance your site's visibility. Some of these services are valuable and well worth the investment, while others are nothing more than scams. This section will help you determine the difference. At times this discussion will seem a bit technical; however, most concepts are fairly straightforward once you get past the technical jargon. Don't worry, I promise I won't try to turn you into a programmer!

Getting a Good Search Engine Listing

GIVEN THAT SEARCH ENGINES reach only a small fraction of the available sites on the Web, how will a search engine find your site? Even when a search engine locates your site, it's no guarantee a potential prospect or client will find you. Your site is a needle in an enormous haystack. Sitting and waiting will not get you found. You must call attention to yourself. But how? Let's first look at some of the approaches to avoid, other approaches that don't work, and questionable practices that might get you labeled as a spammer. Then we'll look at how you or your developer can increase the chances of a directory or a search engine finding you.

THE MAJOR PLAYERS

HERE ARE THE major search engines currently on the Web.

- AltaVista
- Excite
- FAST Search
- Google
- HotBot
- Infoseek
- Lycos
- Magellan
- MSN
- Northern Light
- Planet Search
- WebCrawler
- WebTop

A more complete list with a description of the major search engines and directories is listed in Appendix B.

WHAT YOU SHOULDN'T BELIEVE

◆ **Myth 1.** One of the most common myths about search engines is that most allow advertisers to buy a better position in the search results. This is only completely true at GoTo.com and true to a lesser degree at Ask Jeeves (some e-commerce partners are given preferred placement there—see the Ask Jeeves Editorial Policy). The rest of the major search engines do not sell positions within their main search results areas.

◆ **Myth 2.** Another common myth is that a site's volume of traffic is the primary determinant in whether a site appears on a search engine. It is certainly important, but many very small sites appear frequently on all major search engines and directories. They do so because they have taken the time to design their sites properly and continue to work actively to keep their sites visible to the search engines and current with the directories.

◆ **Myth 3.** How about those firms that "guarantee a top placement" (usually top ten or twenty). Can they really deliver? *No!* It's virtually impossible to guarantee a top twenty placement. Unfortunately, there are "guaranteed top twenty" placement services that charge as much as $2,500 (though most are in the $50 to $100 range). Read the fine print. There are usually so many conditions that it is extremely difficult to collect on these guarantees. It is also difficult to find or understand search engine ratings. These guarantees are simply playing the odds that you won't ask for your money back.

USING KEYWORDS AND PHRASES

NOTE: THE KEYWORD TECHNIQUES described below work for both custom and template sites. Remember that the template site developer is actually providing very little text. Most of what is included in the template is graphics and is ignored by most search engines. If you have a template site, you simply need to be more creative since only certain portions of the content you provide appear on the home page of your site.

A keyword or key phrase is a word or phrase related to the strategy of your Web site. For example, if your strategy is based on benefits marketing, then use words or phrases like 401(k), pension plan, employee benefits, etc.

However, search engines are very stupid! They are going to look through your site and select the words and phrases used most frequently and in key locations throughout. They will then index your site based on these words and phrases *and only these words and phrases.* If you mention that you do "estate planning," but you don't indicate anywhere that you are an "estate planner," your prospect won't find you when they search for an "estate planner."

So, how do you choose what keywords to use? *The most effective way of coming up with keywords is to start thinking like your customer.* If your prospects or clients were going to try to find a site like yours, what terms would they enter in a search engine? Go out (if you haven't already) and search for your competitors' sites. Don't limit yourself to rep offices here; online firms are competitors, as are banks, insurance companies, mutual fund companies, and so on. What words did you use to find them? By the way, don't be surprised if you don't find many competitor sites, particularly rep sites. Most sites are poorly designed for search engine ranking. Now think about the kinds of frequent questions you get from new clients; they may be looking for answers to those questions online as well.

Write down a list of fifty words. Keeping in mind your site's objective and any market niches you are exploiting, choose some of the single words and form them into key phrases such as "long-term savings," "college account," "financial planning services," "estate planning advice," "life insurance quotations," or "stock quotes." This enables the site to rank better on those phrases as opposed to relying on vague keywords such as "planning." It is difficult to have a good ranking on a search engine with such a broad keyword. Keywords like "planning" or "stocks" result in tens of thousands of listings. Aim for a keyword list of around thirty words, and be sure to include your business name, as well as those of any affiliates, such as your broker-dealer.

You need your Web site to be content-rich, with your keywords built into the body of your text. The three main things search engines look for are:

◆ **Keyword prominence and location.** Words that are found at the top of the page are given more weight than those found at the bottom of the page. Focus on the first 1,000 characters of text on your page. The sooner your keywords appear, the better. However, you do need to strike a creative balance here. This is not merely a listing of keywords: You need to entice your visitor into spending time on your site. So don't become too caught up in making the search engines happy at the expense of your site's functionality. Also, take care that you don't get too carried away with graphics. Some search engines have a minimum number of words on the initial page (Lycos requires 100). Remember that text that is converted to graphics to make it more visually appealing or to integrate it with a photo background is no longer seen as text by the search engine.

◆ **Keyword frequency.** Keywords and keyword phrases that are used more often are given more weight. Again, don't get carried away—you can end up with a boring site. Simply be aware of your keywords and phrases and use them as often as possible throughout your site.

◆ **Keyword density.** Search engines look at the density of your keyword phrases relative to the text on your Web site. If your Web site contains 100 words and your keyword phrase is used ten times, your keyword density is 10 percent. Your Web site would (all factors considered) rank higher in the search engine results than a Web site that used the keyword phrase only one time, with a density of only 1 percent. Generally, keyword density should be in the 2 percent to 8 percent range, because search engines will penalize you for using keywords too much! To check your Web site's keyword frequency and density, use http://www.keywordcount.com.

USING DOORWAY PAGES

DOORWAY PAGES? What the heck are those? A doorway page is simply a page created to produce a higher search engine ranking for a particular keyword or set of keywords. These pages act as "doorways" to your site, without the need to redesign or modify content in your current Web site's pages. This is one way to avoid some of the design problems created by trying to use too many keywords and phrases on the initial pages of your site. Using doorway pages allows you to focus the page on one keyword or phrase and give the search engine exactly what it is looking for.

Note: *Although you can obviously have a custom site developer use doorway pages, they also are extremely effective with a template site.* First, you will need to talk to the template site developer to be sure the setup has no special restrictions on doorway page use. Then the developer, an Internet marketing firm, another Web page developer, or even you, using special software, can construct the actual pages.

Why create separate doorway pages? Why not simply include all these keywords and phrases on your site? Well, since each search engine ranks pages differently, it is almost impossible for a single page to rank well on all engines for every possible keyword or phrase. Moreover, your Web site is designed for people, to market your services, assist your clients, and make money. However, the very things that make your site easy to use may make it difficult to search for the search engine. Search engines stumble over things like intense graphics, dynamically generated pages, or a variety of general topics. This is particularly a problem for a template site, since much of the template comes from a database and is dynamically created during the site setup phase. Doorway pages provide a solution.

How many doorway pages do you need? Typically, when targeting ten keywords across five search engines, you will end up with fifty pages pointing to your home page or another section on your site. Do not worry: This isn't unusual. Search engines won't penalize you as long as your doorway pages are professional and honest and so is your submission (avoid the practices listed under "Search Engine Spam" on page 168).

Obviously, creating doorway pages requires some understanding of how the individual search engines rank. Therefore, you have three choices. You can develop this expertise yourself, purchase software that will create doorway pages, or hire someone to do it for you.

Unless you plan to become a Web developer or have lots of free time, I don't believe developing the expertise yourself is a good option. The search engines won't tell you how they search, so the only way to find out is by visiting Web developer sites like internet.com's Web Developer's Library (http://www.stars.com/WDVL/) or chat rooms, or through trial and error.

A couple of programs will do most of the work for you. The first is First Place Software's Web Position Gold (http://www.biz web2000.com/wpa/). This software will generate HTML pages designed to rank near the top of the search results. It also analyzes your existing Web pages and gives advice on how to improve them. It will then submit your pages to the major search engines automatically and report your positions on each search engine for each keyword you are targeting. Finally, it tracks the number of visitors to your site, where they came from, and what keywords they used to find you. All in all, this is a pretty useful piece of software.

PositionWeaver's Gold or Pro is a specialized software program designed specifically to produce doorway pages and can be used in conjunction with Web Position Gold (http://position weaver.com).

Literally thousands of companies will develop doorway pages for you. Two of the better firms (Top Site Indexing and 1 Step Web site Promotions) were mentioned earlier in "How Do I Use Search Services?" in Chapter 5.

USING META TAGS[1]

META TAGS ARE actually part of the HTML code that creates your Web site. If you want to see what this code looks like, simply open any Web site with the MS Internet Explorer Web browser. Then click on View and then Source. What you are seeing is the HTML code that creates the site. Within this code will be meta tags like those described below. The main function of meta tags is to help you increase your search engine placement. The other function is to attract attention and cause a visitor to click through to your Web site from the search engine's results page.

Unless you have a very accommodating template site developer willing to do additional coding for you (unlikely and costly), the use of meta tags is restricted to the custom site developer. So look over your site's HTML code and suggest changes to your custom site developer based on the comments below.

Here are the major types of meta tags, with their HTML coding shown in parentheses:

◆ **Title (<Title>).** The title tag is the most important meta tag, and all too often it is not used properly. This is not the title on your home page but the title that appears in the browser's window— your Web page title. Your title is usually listed as part of the search engine's results. Some search engines give more weight to titles than to body text. Use a descriptive title that contains your keywords; don't use generic phrases such as *home page*.

◆ **Description (<meta name="Description...").** The description tag is the next most important meta tag. Like the title, your description will typically be listed as part of the search engine's results. As with the title, you will have to tread the fine line between creating an effective description that will attract visitors and using one that will rank well in the search engines for your keywords.

To illustrate, let's say a prospect is doing a search using one of the major search engines. When the results of the search appear, the results are a series of Web site links listed in a column. Within each listing both the title and the description meta tag information appears:

> Your Web page title will be displayed here—The description of your Web site will be displayed here... http://www.your-web page.com/

◆ **Keywords (<meta name="Keywords...").** Due to abuse by many Web sites in the past, search engines have reduced the importance of the keywords meta tag when ranking a Web page for keyword relevance. Many have actually even decided to ignore the keywords tag altogether. Although it has declined in significance, it is still an important meta tag to include in your Web pages.

◆ **Copyright (<meta name="Copyright...").** The copyright meta tag, like the two meta tags described below, are hidden. They are not viewable in the search engine results or your Web page. The copyright meta tag is essentially an opportunity for you to enter your company name in the meta tags. Some engines will read this tag, which could result in your company's ranking higher in the engines than it would otherwise.

◆ **Robots (<meta name="Robots...").** The robots tag serves as a set of instructions for the search engines when they visit your Web site. You can tell the search engines to index all of your Web pages, only the ones promoted, or none of your Web pages. This is particularly useful if you have pages of information that might misdirect the indexing function of a search engine (for example, a page on current local events) or if you have a "links" page with useful links that your clients might like but that are unrelated to your site content. This important tag should not be excluded.

◆ **Rating (<meta name="Rating...").** The ratings meta tag will tell the search engines a little more about your Web site—for example, whether it is acceptable for all audiences or for adult audiences only. Some engines will look specifically for this meta tag, so be sure to include it within your Web page.

I suggest you discuss each of these meta tags with your custom site developer before and during the construction of your site. He may be able to suggest some appropriate tags for each of these. Remember, while you may not know exactly how the meta tag functions, you do know much better than the developer the type of prospect you want to attract, so don't be intimidated.

USING OTHER HTML TAGS

AS WITH META TAGS, only a custom site developer can modify your site with these other HTML tags. Check your site's HTML code and meet with your developer to discuss any changes you think are necessary.

◆ **ALT tags**[2]. ALT tags are another chunk of HTML code used in creating your site. If your Web pages use images, image maps, or photos, you should make use of the ALT image tag. ALT image tags are an extension of images that display alternative text for users who cannot read images (such as search engines).

This has the most impact with search engines that index of all your site's text, because you are now providing them with the textual meaning of your graphics. Thus, they can index more content from your Web site. The more images your site contains, the more advantage you have in using the ALT image tag to provide descriptions for search engines. This technique is quite effective, especially for Web sites that have graphics at the top of their pages and for Web sites with a large number of images.

HTML Code: <IMG SRC="URL" ALT="Insert your alternative text here">

◆ **Link tags.** A third piece of HTML code you need to look at is the Link tags. Whenever your developer uses text or an image to link to another page on your site, that's a Link tag. Some search engines weigh the text within a Link more heavily than words found in the regular body text. Finding a Link tag within the HTML code is a bit more difficult because it isn't actually called a Link tag in the code. Instead, it is part of something called an HREF. Therefore, use keywords within the link portion of your HREF tags.

HTML Code: <A HREF="pagename.htm">keyword phrase</A>

Don't forget to have the page named with a keyword phrase as well (see "pagename.htm" above). Separate multiple keywords with a dash, such as variable-annuity.htm as opposed to variableannuity.

◆ **Header tags.** A common mistake in coding is for the developer to put your keyword phrases in font tags and not in header tags. Headings are the larger print on a page. Search engines often consider header text particularly important, and they pay little attention to keyword phrases in font tags. So check the header tags to be sure they have your keywords included. You should make sure your developer's first header tag is the same as your meta tag title (see "meta tags" on page 163).

HTML Code: <H1>Web page title</H1>

PROMOTING LINKS TO YOUR SITE

WHILE HAVING A LOT of links on your site to other sites can be cumbersome and a compliance nightmare, having a lot of links from other sites to you is just the reverse. The number of pages that have links to you can influence your listing in some search engines (and is of little compliance concern, though the wording or image used on the other site for the link to your site needs to be reviewed). Search engines can determine how many other Web sites link to your Web site, and some will give your Web site a boost in the results when a lot of pages link to you.

Encourage people to link to your site by providing banners or other linking graphics for them to use on their site. Be sure to provide detailed instructions on how to link to your Web site. Find out where your competitors are linked and start there. Strategic links are also a good source of additional traffic to your Web site. Target Web sites that have some real affinity to yours. For example, some of the financial service industry publications now have a place for rep Web site links. If, say, you are a servicing agent for a client's retirement plan, propose a link on the company's 401(k) site.

CHOOSING YOUR OWN URL (WEB SITE ADDRESS)

◆ **Use keywords in your URL.** Search engines give more weight to a name like www.xyzadvisors.com/financial_planning.htm than to www.mypage.com/page.htm. Make it a habit to include keywords in all your sub pages where you can. Separate keywords with a dash, underscore, or a slash: www.domain.com/life-insurance. htm. Robots and spiders cannot differentiate between attached words.

◆ **Get your own domain name.** This gives your site more credibility than user pages on an ISP, and some search engines consider this. Many of the larger Web hosting services will offer you your own domain name as part of their service (they will usually handle the registration for you). You can do it yourself by going to Network Solutions' WHOIS site (http://www.network solutions.com/cgi-bin/whois/whois). Here you can test combinations of names until you find one that is available and register it online.

You might want to get your own domain name for no other reason than portability. If you ever need to change hosts and you do not have your own domain name, you will have to change your Web address. It would be a shame to build up your traffic and then lose it because you cannot keep your Web address.

SEARCH ENGINE SITE REVIEWS

GETTING YOUR WEB SITE REVIEWED by a search engine can have a positive impact on your ranking in search results. This is not as difficult as it might seem at first. Some search engines provide top ranking for a Web site that has been found to provide valuable information. If your site has truly useful information on it or is unique is some way, submit it. Custom sites are more likely to offer the kind of uniqueness that a search engine is looking for, although the quality of content on a template might qualify if it is valuable enough.

To submit a site for review, you need only go to that search engine's home page and look for the appropriate submission area. Note that not every search engine has a review process.

UPDATE YOUR WEB SITE

DO NOT LET YOUR SITE get stagnant. Not only is it good business practice to give your visitors a reason to return, but your Web site's position on search engines can actually be influenced by the frequency of page updates. The search engine's spider is capable of determining how often you make changes and will give you a higher position in the list if you make frequent updates. You need to make changes at least every other month.

Once you've made your changes, resubmit your Web site. WARNING! If your Web site already has a great ranking on a search engine, do *not* resubmit your site. The search engine algorithm might have changed, and you could actually drop in the rankings.

To test your site ranking, check out Top10Affiliates Search Engine Position Analyzer (http://www.top10affiliates.com/search_engine_submission/submit.shtml). It is helpful to know how well your site is ranking with the biggest search engines. If your site does not appear in the first fifty entries, then you can pretty much expect very few people to find it.

What You Shouldn't Do

SEARCH ENGINE SPAM

LISTED BELOW ARE THE most common abuses by overly enthusiastic, misguided, or simply dishonest marketers. Major violations with these tactics will get you labeled as a spammer. The impact for a site like yours can be disastrous. The search engines or directories in question will ban your site from their indexes, and you will cease to exist as far as the public is concerned.

There is no reason to panic. Note that I said "major violations." The people who run the search engines know that the very nature of your Web site can produce pages that appear to be spam to the engine. They also know that their search engines are not smart enough to distinguish between those that are spamming and those that simply appear to be. Thus, they are not going to ban your site from their search engine because of a mistake. Instead, they will only penalize the rankings of the offending pages—not the entire site. However, if you aggressively spam them (using the techniques described below), flooding their engine with spam pages, they *will* ban your entire site.

Therefore, if you're having a custom site built for you, make sure your developer isn't using any of these approaches to market your site. If you are using an unfamiliar template site developer, I'd check for these problems as well.

◆ **Keyword stuffing.** This is the repeated use of a word to increase its frequency on a page. Search engines now have the ability to analyze a page and determine whether the frequency is above a "normal" level in proportion to the rest of the words in the document.

◆ **Invisible text.** Some Webmasters stuff keywords at the bottom of a page and make their text color the same as that of the page background. This is also detectable by the engines.

◆ **Tiny text.** This is similar to invisible text but uses tiny, illegible text.

◆ **Page redirects.** Some engines, especially Infoseek, do not like pages that take the user to another page without the user's intervention. To the visitor, a page appears and almost immediately is replaced by another page.

◆ **Meta tag stuffing.** Do not use your keywords in the meta tags more than once, and do not use keywords that are unrelated to your site's content. A meta tag is part of the HTML code (see page 163).

◆ **Unrelated words.** Never use keywords that do not apply to your site's content.

◆ **Too many similar doorways.** Doorway pages (also known as gateway or bridge pages) are specifically created for a keyword phrase or phrases and optimized for a particular search engine. Do not create huge numbers of doorway pages with very similar keywords.

◆ **Too many submissions.** Do not submit the same page more than once on the same day to the same search engine. Do not submit more than the allowed number of pages per engine per day or week. Each engine has a limit on how many pages you can manually submit to it using its online forms. Currently, these are the limits: AltaVista, one to ten pages per day; HotBot, fifty pages per day; Excite, twenty-five pages per week; and Infoseek, fifty pages per day, but unlimited when using e-mail submissions (check with the other search engines for their limits).

◆ **Identical pages.** Do not submit virtually identical pages; that is, do not simply duplicate a Web page, give the copies different file names, and submit them all. This will be interpreted as an attempt to flood the engine. This is called *search engine spamming.* If your submissions are interpreted this way, the search engine can refuse to list your site and blacklist you to other search engines. To trigger this response, however, the offense has to be quite blatant. A few identical pages won't get you blacklisted—but submitting ten, twenty, or a hundred will get you booted.

◆ **Code swapping.** Do not optimize a page for top ranking and then swap another page in its place once a top ranking is achieved.

◆ **Sending doorways to directories.** Do not submit doorways to submission directories like Yahoo!

OTHER QUESTIONABLE PRACTICES

◆ **Flooding Usenet newsgroups.** Sending redundant or irrelevant advertisements to Usenet newsgroups is frustrating to other Internet users. Certainly, there are times when it's appropriate to send a message describing your Web site to a newsgroup. Some are even set up for this purpose. However, flooding newsgroups with repeated messages in order to get your Web site noticed is not the way to do it.

◆ **Flooding chat rooms or forums.** Unfortunately, it is becoming popular for marketers to advertise through online chat rooms using programs to flood rooms with messages or automatically send a message to every user connected to that service. These messages slow the host's server and become very annoying very quickly—and are rarely effective.

Getting a Good Directory Listing

THESE ARE THE major online directories:

- ◆ Yahoo!
- ◆ About.com
- ◆ Open Directory Project
- ◆ Snap
- ◆ Google Web Directory

A more complete list with descriptions of the major search engines and directories is given in Appendix B.

DIRECTORY CONSIDERATIONS

WHILE THERE ARE only a few important directories, they are *very* important. Yahoo! and the Open Directory Project may be the most important search engines out there, so be sure to do a good job submitting to them.

Directory submission is very different from search engine submissions. Remember, when you submit to a directory site you are actually asking a *real person* to evaluate your site and to publish your link and description in one or more categories. Ask yourself, "What is the category that best fits my site?" In addition, "Does my site deserve a placement in that category?"

This is not as easy as it seems. First, there are usually a huge number of categories to choose from. Some of these categories could perfectly describe your site or services, but they are not very popular. Others might only vaguely match your services but are extremely popular. Some directories determine the categories for your site directly from your site description, so you need to be careful to include your categories as part of your site description. To look at a directory's categories, you have two methods of attack. You can either play client and surf through the category links on a directory, looking for the logical place you would expect to find your site, or search for your competitors' listings (as with the search engines) and look at the categories under which they were listed.

Second, the person reviewing your site gets hundreds of submissions like yours every day. He or she wants to make a quick categorization and doesn't want to waste time. *Your site is unlikely to get more than a few minutes of review.* At that point, the reviewer is going to decide whether your selection of categories and/or your description is accurate and whether your site is good enough to be listed. Other categories or description changes may be suggested. If your site is turned down or you're required to make changes, you will need to resubmit. Resubmitting can be difficult and can take a long time.

So be prepared. Your site must be complete and very, very relevant for the category you target. Besides the category choice, you may need to submit your URL, the site title, a description, and some keywords.

Spend time on your description, because it is critical to building site traffic from directories. You should have at least two descriptions. One should be short—fewer than 25 words—and the other should be as long as necessary, up to about 100 words. Some directories accept only short descriptions. Others will take descriptions of virtually any size. Some take both a short and a long description. You need to be prepared for both types. You may even be asked to shorten your short description for some submissions.

Other Ways to Help Clients Find You

ANNOUNCEMENTS

BELOW ARE VARIOUS TYPES of announcement services. These are an excellent way for you to begin building traffic to your site. However, remember that this is a slow process and will require ongoing attention.

◆ **DirectoryGuide** (http://www.directoryguide.com) is a free service that has an extensive catalog of search engines and directories that accept Web site announcements. After reviewing more than 1,000 sites, the service selected 400 that it believes provide the best promotion value to Web marketers.

◆ **Multimedia Marketing Group's WebStep TOP 100** (http://www.mmgco.com/top100.html) features links to the best 100 places that will list your Web site free.

◆ **Netscape's What's New page** (http://home.netscape.com/net center/newaward.html?cp=newdepart) lists new launches selected by Netscape. Submissions are heavily reviewed, so you're not guaranteed acceptance.

◆ **Yahoo!'s What's New Pages** (http://dir.yahoo.com/computers_ and_internet/internet/world_wide_Web/searching_the_Web/ indices_to_Web_documents/what_s_new) links to announcement services and other What's New pages.

SUBMITTING YOUR SITE'S FEATURES OR SECTIONS INDIVID-UALLY

ONE OF THE GREATEST FEATURES of the Web is its ability to bore down to the specific information a user is looking for. Your site isn't an entity; it is a collection of features and information. For example, do you have an e-mail discussion list you could promote separately by submitting it to directories such as Liszt (http://www.liszt.com) and Tile.Net (http://www.tile.net)? Focusing in on your site's features and sections can increase your submission options. Such features as seminars, bulletin boards, chat rooms, educational articles, newsletters, or e-zines can all be promoted independently of your site.

INFORMATIVE WEB SITE

DEVELOPING A WEB SITE that talks about your product or service is fine, but providing additional useful information is even better. For example, let's say you are ready to develop a site that promotes your financial planning services. You have a great service to sell, but everyone and their brother is offering financial planning. If, in addition, you work out an arrangement with a local attorney and local CPA to offer a broader range of services through a single site, you have made your site more informative and attractive. In turn, it will be easier to get other sites to link to you. The more sites that link to you, the higher your Web site's placement in the search engines.

REGISTER WITH SAFESURF OR RSACI

SOME COMPANIES SUCH AS SAFESURF (http://www.safesurf.com) and RSACi (http://www.icra.org) are filtering out Web sites that are not registered . This means if your Web site does not have a rating, it can not be viewed in some cases. You might find that some large corporation is blocking out your site.

CROSS-PROMOTIONS

ONE OF THE BEST WAYS to drive traffic to your site is to integrate your normal marketing with your Web site. You can't expect to market your Web site exclusively online. Even with the Internet revolution, people still use multiple channels to get their information. If you want your site to be successful, you must fully integrate it with your other marketing efforts. When you send out a mailer or place an ad, include your Web site address. When you're on the phone with prospects or clients, invite them to visit your site. Give your site address when asking for referrals. Put your Web address on your letterhead and business cards. Include your address in your radio or TV spots.

Make sure your URL is displayed prominently when you give a seminar. Include it in your on-hold message and put it on your faxes. Make sure your sales brochures include a section promoting the use of your site. Focus part of your marketing strategy exclusively on promoting your Web site. Once you have done all this, then you can concentrate on marketing your site online.

USING DATABASES TO PULL EVERYTHING TOGETHER

SUPPOSE YOUR NEXT PHONE CALL were from a prospect who would not give his name, address, or any details about his financial situation. However, he would like you to develop a financial plan for him. How could you go any further with this potential client without background information and the ability to contact him?

Similarly, if your site is not collecting and retaining information about your visitors, how can you target their needs? Yet many rep sites have no data collection capability other than a hit counter (usually provided by the Web host) and an e-mail link. This is usually because their owners didn't take time to think through the purpose of their site or relied on the Web developer to provide this capability.

You cannot provide good service if you don't know

when or why your clients are using your site. You certainly can't sell your services to new prospects if you can't even figure out their names. Your site needs some form of information collection capability, and you need to store that data in some type of database. The database can reside online or separate from the Internet. It is even possible for the database to reside with a third party. In fact, most template Web sites, discussed earlier, are database-driven. If you plan to use databases, the first step is to determine what kind of data you need to capture.

Identifying and Capturing Information Online

SOMEWHERE ON YOUR SITE you need to incorporate a data collection tool. This can be part of a log-in procedure or simply a portion of the site that visitors can go to if they wish. How you collect the data depends on the answers to two questions: How important is the information to you? And how willing are you to restrict the number of visitors to your site in order to collect it? To answer these questions, you need to go back to your site's goals and marketing plan.

CONTACT INFORMATION

THE MOST IMPORTANT DATA to collect is contact information about prospects and clients. Without contact information, you have no way to follow up on client questions or prospect inquiries. Do not make the common mistake of assuming that an e-mail link on your site will provide you with this information (i.e., the visitor clicks on an e-mail link on your site, and the standard blank e-mail form loads from his browser).

There are a number of problems with this approach. First, because the standard e-mail form contains only "to," "from," and "message" boxes, you are very limited in the information you can collect. For example, the "from" box does not contain a name; it contains the sender's e-mail address. This is helpful if when you open the e-mail it says bobjones@aol.com, but useless if it says bj10@aol.com. You can reply to the sender, but you still have no idea who is asking you the question. You are also not going to consistently get information like addresses or phone numbers because there is no place for these on the standard e-mail form.

In addition, the "message" field is not mandatory, so unless the visitor fills it in, your "message" box will be blank. Thus, you will have no way to determine whether this message is from your Web site or what it is about. Also keep in mind that because sending you an e-mail is voluntary, the information you collect via e-mail is incomplete. A number of visitors to your site may find something of interest but either choose not to send an e-mail or simply not see the e-mail option.

However, the most serious limitation is that you may have no permanent record of any information that the visitor sends you in this e-mail. Should you need to reach this person in the future, you will have no contact information readily available unless you saved the initial e-mail. This is where a database becomes very important to Web marketing.

You are going to have to make some decisions regarding when to ask for the information you need and how much information to ask for. Here is a sample set of typical contact information questions (those in bold are normally mandatory):

First Name _____ Middle Initial _____
Last Name _____
Home Street Address _____
City _____ **State**____ Zip Code _____
Home Phone (including area code) _____
Home E-mail Address _____
Business Name _____
Business Street Address _____
City _____ State____ Zip Code _____
Business Phone (including area code) _____
Business Phone Extension _____
Business Fax (Including area code) _____
Business E-mail Address _____
Business Web Site Address _____

ASKING THE RIGHT QUESTIONS

MUCH OF WHAT YOU ASK will depend on the type of site you develop and the marketing plan that it supports. However, there are some general guidelines in developing database questions.

◆ **Make sure you have a purpose for your question.** Don't ask a question just because it would be interesting to know. The information you ask for should be required in order for you sell or support a particular product or service.

◆ **Keep your questions short.** Long questions tend to become confusing and have a lower response rate.

◆ **Keep the number of questions to a minimum.** There is no set number or guideline since this depends on the product or service to which these questions relate. However, try not to ask more than ten questions in any single Web site section.

◆ **Databases deal better with objective questions than subjective questions.** Structure most of your questions as fill-in-the-blank, multiple choice, true-false, or ranking scale (1 to 5, like to dislike, etc.). Leave a few open-ended subjective questions at the end if they seem appropriate.

◆ **Use online forms.** It is much easier for the user to answer questions on the site than to list their answers in an e-mail.

ONLINE FORMS

ONLINE FORMS ALLOW YOU to ask specific questions in a preformatted form. There are several basic types of online forms; Java, HTML, and PDF are the most common. The Java and HTML forms can include drop-down menus, check boxes, and radio buttons that allow the user to quickly answer questions with little typing. These forms will look best in the user's browser since the form automatically configures for the size of the browser frame and the resolution of the monitor. In addition, if you plan to use the information you capture through the online form in a database, this approach works best.

PDF forms are best for completing a preprinted form online, because the version of the forms printed by the user is identical to the preprinted form. PDF forms can be configured either to be printed and then completed or to be completed online (however, the online capabilities are more limited than those of Java or HTML).

CLIENTS

SINCE YOU ALREADY HAVE a relationship with a client, you have more freedom in the questions you can ask them. However, they are going to be less willing to complete contact information questions since they perceive (and rightly so) that you already have that information on them.

There are a number of ramifications to online client data-gathering. First, clients are more likely to complete many of the typical administrative forms online if you make this process as painless as possible. This can be a great time-saver for you and your clients. Clients are also more willing to complete mandatory questions if they can see the value of the service, support, or product they are getting in exchange. Thus, be sure you remind them what they are getting in return.

Clients are also likely to appreciate efforts to integrate your client management software with your Web site, since you can complete portions of these forms for them. (See "Using and Integrating the Information You Collect," on the following page.) Given that clients have a higher level of trust in you and thus in your site, they are also more likely than unknown site visitors to complete in-depth online forms, such as online planning or risk-assessment questionnaires and so on.

PROSPECTS

PROSPECTS, ON THE OTHER HAND, are going to be more distrustful of giving out personal or financial information on a rep Web site. A good approach is to ask for only the minimum contact information you need to communicate with them. The choice to communicate this information with you should always be theirs (as with clients, remind them of why you need this information).

Then, periodically give them opportunities to receive free value-added services from you or on your site if they give you additional information. Giving access to online financial planning software or a client newsletter are excellent ways to accomplish this goal.

Using and Integrating
the Information You Collect

EVEN IF YOU HAVE a great Web site that allows you to collect reams of valuable information on prospects and clients, it is pretty useless unless you can do more than just print out the data. This section shows how you can make your Web site more personalized and responsive to your clients' needs by integrating that data.

The template Web sites mentioned earlier also illustrate another level of database use: database integration. As a template Web-site purchaser, you can configure your site (within limits) to fit your needs. Your site doesn't actually exist until you complete all the setup questions, then create the site in real time based on the profile you've developed. This is database integration.

What distinguishes database integration is that information collected in the database is used to modify the site. Most Web sites today are "static," meaning their content is prewritten and waiting to be accessed on a server. These types of pages change only when a new version of the page is programmed and uploaded to the Internet.

Through database integration, however, the content of a page is actually stored in a database. This means that a Web site's pages don't even exist until the information is requested. Because fields in a database can be added to, deleted, and modified online, these "dynamic" pages are generated in real time.

Database integration can produce some powerful applications that, depending on your site's goals, may or may not be appropriate for your Web site. Some examples include

◆ Password-protected log-in pages that check against an authorized user list before granting access

◆ Updatable product information pages that can be edited and updated through a Web browser

◆ News, newsletter, or announcement forums that enable you to update information on your site online in real time or post your changes and schedule when those updates will appear

◆ Storefront solutions that allow you to sell your services online and collect payment via e-commerce

◆ Catalog-oriented pages that enable users to search for specific products or services through a variety of filters, such as stock or mutual fund screeners or risk-assessment screens

◆ Personalized pages with stored client preferences for each client who enters your site

◆ Automated and customized e-mail follow-up based on visitor Web site selections

Although these are powerful applications, they also require more programming time and carry a higher development cost. This type of site also requires you to have or create a database that can exchange information with your Web site and then maintain it.

Database integration can be used with some template sites, but this type of integration is normally beyond the reach of an individual adviser site. However, some broker-dealers or carriers offer customized template sites that will integrate with the company's back-office or clearing-firm databases. Thus, if you plan on extensive use of database integration, you will probably need a custom site.

Also, be aware that if you incorporate database integration into your site, you also need to spend more time developing doorway pages, since search engines have difficulty dealing with database-driven sites.

ONLINE CLIENT MANAGEMENT SYSTEM

THE MOST SEAMLESS INTEGRATION of a rep Web site and a client database is simply moving your entire client management system online. This allows an exchange of information between your client management database and your Web site. Thus, any contact with your Web site is recorded in your client management system. You know the identity of the prospects or clients who enter your Web site and what they do while they are there. If a prospect or client requests assistance, his entire request is moved to your tickler file. If an online transaction or client account inquiry is made, your client management system has a record of it. The system will also track and manage any e-mail or regular-mail marketing you do. This approach is still very new, but a number of companies are developing systems like this.

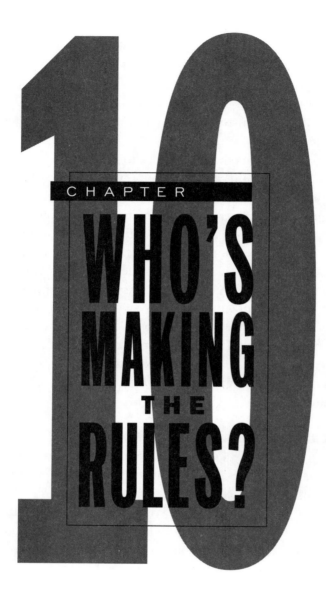

CHAPTER

10

WHO'S MAKING THE RULES?

THE INTERNET HAS CHANGED everything, from the way in which we do business to how we buy books and conduct research and even how we sell securities. The sudden appearance of the Internet came as a shock to financial regulators. Their neat, well-ordered world, where securities advertising, marketing, sales, and processing moved along predictable channels with known players, disappeared literally overnight.

In the dawn of this information age, the opportunities for promoting yourself on the Web have seemingly outstripped the ability of the securities rulemaking authorities to create rules for this new form of commerce. Unfortunately, this has left you (the financial professional) confused about how to promote your business on the Internet without running afoul of the regulators.

Unfortunately, at this point, each regulatory agency and governmental body has a different interpretation of communications on the Internet. In addition, although some practices may be perfectly legal, each broker-dealer creates its own rules and regulations—and some of these are more stringent than what the regulators have in place. It is probably not news to you that before creating any form of communication, you need to check with your firm's compliance department to ensure that it is permissible.

So what are the new rules of securities sales in the age of the Internet? Let's look at several new forms of communication resulting from the explosion in Internet technologies. Web sites, chat rooms, interactive online seminars, and e-mail have expanded our means of communication exponentially. To understand which rules apply to your communications, you must first look at your registration and then consider the type of communication you will be engaged in.

Registered Representatives

REGISTERED REPRESENTATIVES are held to the standards of the National Association of Securities Dealers. The NASD has made it clear that a registered representative's responsibilities when communicating via the Internet are the same as when communicating using traditional methods, whether via written communication or face-to-face.

The NASD considers communications disseminated without control over who receives the information—for instance, Web sites and bulletin board postings—to be advertisements. Likewise, material that is distributed to specific customers or prospects—such as in a group e-mail—is defined as sales literature. Correspondence is material that is disseminated to a single customer or prospect. Thus, an individual e-mail would be considered correspondence. In October 1999 the NASD proposed changes to these definitions that may later affect which rules apply to the different Web-related media.

Regardless of which type of Web communication a financial services professional is involved in, it is important to remember that he or she will be held to the same standards as in more traditional com-

munications. The NASD requires all advertisements and sales literature to be approved by signature or initial of a registered principal
prior to use. This means that Web sites, group e-mail, bulletin board
postings, and so on may not be available to the public until approved.

Certain communications must be filed with the NASD advertising regulation department within ten days of first use or ten days
prior to use, depending on the type of security being advertised.
In general, advertisements and sales literature mentioning mutual
funds, variable contracts, and unit investment trusts; advertisements regarding government securities, collateralized mortgage
obligations, and direct participation programs; and advertisements
and educational materials concerning options must be filed with
the NASD. The NASD has taken the position that the mention of
any of these securities outside of a list of products and services
necessitates this filing.

The NASD advertising regulation department charges $75 for
up to ten pages or minutes of review, with an additional charge of
$10 per page or minute thereafter. Since some Web sites have
many more than ten pages and some Web marketing approaches
require multiple Web sites, it may be more cost-effective to create
a site that does not require NASD review or use material that has
already been filed. Note that some broker-dealers may require you
to wait for the NASD review, so check with your broker-dealer in
advance. The Advertising Regulation Department does offer an
expedited review, which costs $500 for ten pages/minutes and $25
for each page or minute thereafter. Obviously, you should allow
enough lead time in planning your site to avoid the need for an
expedited review.

Registered Investment Advisors

REGISTERED INVESTMENT ADVISORS and their representatives,
whether registered at the SEC or state level, should ensure that
any Internet-based communications accurately reflect what is stat-
ed in their Form ADV, disclosure brochures, and client agreements. The Investment Advisers Act of 1940 sets forth the guidelines for advertisements by investment advisers, and these apply to
the Internet as well.

Specifically, the SEC prohibits investment advisers and their affiliates from referring to or employing any testimonials. In addition, investment advisers may not refer to past recommendations of an adviser that were or would have been profitable to any person, unless the adviser adds specific disclosures.

Investment advisers are also prohibited from implying that any charts, graphs, or other device (this includes those slick online stock and fund screeners) could be used to determine what securities to buy or sell or when to buy or sell them. Last, at the risk of stating the obvious, advisers should avoid any untrue statements or misleading statements.

WEB SITES

GUESS WHAT? Web sites are considered advertisements, and because they are available in every state, they may be considered solicitations in all fifty states. Thus, all sites need to go through these compliance steps:

◆ Your new site will need to be reviewed by your compliance department, and any subsequent changes to your site content, such as updates or additions, will need to be reviewed.

◆ Your compliance department should review any links to other sites (this includes content changes on existing links). Remember that the NASD considers any material on these linked sites that is exaggerated, promissory, inflammatory, or misleading a violation. Note: A disclosure page on leaving your site (e.g. "You are now leaving the joe_rep.com site") does not protect you.

◆ Your Web site should not go live until you have received permission from your compliance department. Not only do you need to be aware of this when you are developing your own site, you need to make sure your developer uses a developmental site that is not accessible from the Internet. Tip: If you can see it online without a password, someone else can find it with a search engine.

◆ You need to list the states in which you are licensed to do business. Remember that anyone anywhere, even outside the United States, can view your site. Most states have found two general methods acceptable for preventing the implication of solicitation without proper licensing. One option is to include a fire-wall page that prevents clients residing in states in which you are not licensed from advancing to the next pages.

Another option is to include disclaimer language on each page that informs prospects of the states in which you are properly registered to offer products or services. Of course, if you actually plan on transacting business or providing personalized advice without using one of these screening options, plan on registering in all fifty states. This is not an impossible task, but it is time-consuming and expensive. Because each state has its own interpretations of registration and licensing requirements, it is important to consult with your individual firm's compliance department for guidance.

◆ Any discussion of mutual funds, variable annuities, limited partnerships, government securities, collateralized mortgage obligations (CMOs), or unit investment trusts (UITs) requires filing with the NASD. This is a good reason to use materials developed by a third party that have been previously reviewed by the NASD. Your broker-dealer may have these approvals on file already.

◆ You will need to maintain a Web site file, like your advertising file, with a printed copy of all your pages, links, and subsequent updates.

HYPERLINKS

LINKS TO OTHER WEB SITES should be clearly labeled. There should be no implication that you endorse a Web site or that you are offering the information on the linked site. It is also important to review the material on the linked site, because you may be held responsible for the information. Many broker-dealers require that their compliance department review the linked sites.

CHAT ROOMS

PARTICIPATION IN A CHAT ROOM may be considered participation in a public forum, and as such requires financial professionals to remember the communication rules. In addition, participants in chat rooms must recognize that when discussing investments in this atmosphere, it is impossible to verify what audience is receiving the information. *Therefore, it is unsuitable and possibly dangerous to make any investment recommendation or offer investment advice in a chat room.* Licensed individuals, whether acting anonymously or in their professional capacity, always must be cautious about communicating with the public.

Chat room communications, as with all communications, should be based on principles of fair dealing and good faith and should provide a sound basis for evaluating the facts. You should avoid exaggerated, unwarranted, or misleading statements. Promissory language or inflammatory language that invokes strong emotions should also be avoided. Suitability and recommendation issues should also be considered. The NASD requires very specific disclosures when making recommendations, and these disclosures must be included if a Web communication makes an overt or implied recommendation. All information within the communication should be current. And remember, depending on the type of communication, additional rules may also apply.

RECORD-KEEPING RESPONSIBILITIES

INTERNET COMMUNICATIONS are subject to the same record-keeping requirements as other communications with the public. Depending on your registration, you may be required to maintain files of all communications and copies of all changes to your Web site. It is advisable to print a copy of your site and maintain it in a file sorted by date. This will enable you to reproduce your entire site for any given day, should a regulator or client question the information that was available at any particular time. You don't need to print a copy of your entire Web site every day—only when the information changes.

In general, although the regulatory area is still evolving, the reality is that the compliance concerns are the same as the ones you face with traditional marketing. For further information and updates on pending regulation, you may want to check out www.nasd.com or www.sec.gov.

CONCLUSION

THE ONLINE REVOLUTION isn't so much a threat to you as it is an opportunity and an invitation. There is a future for the financial adviser in this world of the online investor—but only for those bold enough to change the way they do business. Mainspring, in a recent study,[1] found that "while individual investors historically needed brokers to execute transactions as well as provide advice, they now disproportionately rely on brokers for counsel and personalization of investment decisions." They also found that over 90 percent of stockbrokers say the Internet enhances their productivity. Mainspring found that the Internet has created the following:

◆ A new marketing channel and better tools to prioritize and to follow up on leads

◆ Informative resources to facilitate counsel and

decision-making with clients

◆ Clients who are overwhelmed by the wealth of information now available to them

The opportunity is now; you need to take advantage of it. However, you do have time if you use it wisely. This change is not going to happen overnight. Many of the Internet technologies mentioned in this book are still in their infancy, and adoption of the Web by the general public, while growing at an incredible rate, still has a way to go. There will be many frustrations and setbacks with this new medium. Count on it. However, this is where the future is leading. Fund companies, insurance carriers, and broker-dealers are rapidly becoming cyberready, if they aren't already. Your prospects and clients either are or will shortly be moving online. Many of your competitors are already making this move. Don't let them leave you behind. It will become increasingly difficult for the financial services professional to do business using only non-Internet-based technologies. You have only three choices: You can lead, you can follow, or you can get out of the business!

If you learn nothing else from this book, learn this: Don't wait! Sure, most of your prospects and clients may even prefer to use traditional channels, and the Internet will never completely replace these channels, but you still need to start now. You need time to understand this new Internet medium and time to adapt your practice to its use. Learn to use the new rules of the virtual road. Unburden yourself of the common misconceptions about the Web. Keep this book to use as your road map, and with some innovative thinking, you too can build a successful online practice.

To stay abreast of current developments and ideas, visit www.movingyourpracticeonline.com. If you have comments or suggestions, please pass them along.

APPENDIX A

ONLINE MARKETING PLANS

CONSTRUCTING AN ONLINE MARKETING PLAN is a process that follows many of the same steps you used to develop a traditional marketing or business plan. Actually, the result you obtain may be quite similar. In fact, the principal reason to go through this exercise is to break your thinking out of the old paradigm and to allow you to create new ways to integrate this additional medium into your overall marketing.

So be careful not to fall back into old familiar patterns just because they're familiar. Keep asking yourself questions like "Could I do that mailing with an e-mail?" "Do I really need to visit that client in person?" "Do they need to fill out a printed form?" "Can this presentation work online?"

Remember also, though, that the Web is not the solution for all marketing and service questions. What you are doing right now might be the best solution. The Internet has limitations, so don't get carried away.

Below is an outline of the major sections contained in an Internet marketing plan, along with some comments regarding the contents of each section and, in some cases, links to sources of additional information. Following is a sample plan for a customer service strategy, as described in Chapter 1.

Model for an Online Marketing Plan

THE CUSTOMER

THIS SECTION DESCRIBES your target audience, the Internet environment, and the market environment in which you do business.

◆ **Market segmentation variables.** Research your market from your experience, client base, and external sources. Describe the average or the top 20 percent of your clients (and potential prospects). Develop your client and prospect profile according to age, gender, income group, and Internet literacy.

Look also at psychometric measures like culture and peer groups. Determine whether your clients are decision makers, influencers, buyers, or gatekeepers with regard to purchases. Look at their geographic distribution.

The U.S. Census site (http://www.census.gov) and the Market-Research.com site (http://www.marketresearch.com) can be helpful.

◆ **General Internet user statistics.** Use the CommerceNet Research Center (http://www.commerce.net/research) and the Yahoo! Marketing and Advertising section on online Internet research services (http://dir.yahoo.com/Business_and_Economy/Companies/Marketing_and_Advertising/Internet/Market_Research/) to find out the latest on Internet growth and use.

◆ **Target market definition.** Take your own research and the above information to formally define your Internet target market. This may be quite different from your traditional marketing target.

◆ **External marketing environment.** Look at the big picture. Ask yourself the following questions:

— What political (local or national elections, new pending legislation, etc.), economic (market predictions, large layoffs, a new employer, etc.), social/cultural (baby boomer clients getting ready for retirement, influx of foreign workers, etc.), or technological (cable carrier adds Internet service, new low-cost ISP, etc.) changes could affect your market?

— Who are your existing and potential Internet competitors, and what are they doing?

— Who has Web sites?

— Who uses e-mail?

◆ **SWOT analysis.** What are your strengths, weaknesses, opportunities, and threats?

Note: Most opportunities and threats are derived from your strengths and weaknesses, so be sure your assessment is honest. This is not a feel-good document—no one but you need see it.

Out of this list, which are the critical success factors? Which ones will be most critical to the success or failure of your Internet marketing?

THE PLAN

◆ **Online goal.** Here is where you describe what you want to accomplish online. Start by writing out every idea that surfaced as a critical success factor above. Distill these to a single, concise statement of not more than three or four lines. Don't be surprised if this takes longer than any other section to complete. Expect that you will go through a number of revisions before you get something you are comfortable with. Don't skimp here; this single statement, if used properly, will do more to keep you on track and successful than almost anything else you do.

◆ **Objectives.** Now that you've got what you want to accomplish in general, begin writing short, concise statements of the specific things you need to do to accomplish your goal. Note: No matter how potentially lucrative or successful, if a proposed marketing or service idea doesn't meet your online goal, DON'T DO IT! If you persist in adopting new online marketing approaches just because they are new, your marketing will rapidly become unfocused and ineffective.

Each objective you construct should be time-limited and measurable. Someone should always be assigned responsibility for the objective. For example, "By April 1, 2001, I will implement a short monthly e-mail to all my existing clients with links back to my Web site for more information on specific subjects." This is preferable to "Start sending out e-mails."

◆ **Online promotional and service plans.** If your objectives include using online channels for sales to either new or existing clients and/or service to existing clients, you need to describe in a few short paragraphs how you expect each of these to work. What online channels will you be using? How will you integrate this with your existing marketing and service efforts?

The Web-Site Development Plan

STRUCTURE

CONSTRUCT A WIRING DIAGRAM for your site. You will need this to help you visualize the site and to aid in explaining it to others. Even a simple site can be very complicated to explain. Create this diagram even when you are using a template site constructed and maintained by others—you still need this aid to do your planning (ask your site developer to put a diagram together for you to save you time). Continue to update this diagram as your site develops and changes.

COMPUTING/HOSTING ENVIRONMENT

WHERE WILL THE SITE be hosted? On what kind of server will it be hosted? What backup systems are available? What kind of capacity and access speed will your site have?

CONTENT AND DATABASE MAINTENANCE

HOW WILL YOU maintain the site? Will you need special software? How quickly can updates be posted? Will you need to integrate with an existing database? How will you maintain compliance oversight on changes?

E-COMMERCE

IF YOU PLAN TO ALLOW purchases from your site, how will client security be maintained? Will you require special software?

CUSTOMER SERVICE

IF YOU PLAN TO service customers from your site, what services will you provide? Will they require special programming?

Project Resources, Budget, and Timeline

PROMOTION AND SERVICE CALENDAR

DEVELOP A CALENDAR for the entire year that shows both online and traditional promotional and service events.

◆ **Write an online marketing budget.** Associate a cost estimate with each of your online activities and integrate this estimate with your overall marketing budget (track online costs separately, though). Include any technology purchases, lease, hosting, or development costs.

◆ **Action plans.** For major projects necessary for you to accomplish your objectives, you will need to develop an action plan. Note that I said "major," not "all" projects. Develop a full-blown action plan only if a project has a significant impact on your budget or has the potential for a dramatic impact on your production. Each action plan should include the following:

—What will be done
—When it will be done
—Who will do it (include any third parties involved)
—Projected cash-flow statement (budget)
—Periodic evaluation of progress

Sample Online Marketing Plan

NOTE: THE EXAMPLE THAT APPEARS on the following pages uses fictitious data and is meant to be used only for form and style reference. (See "XYZ Advisory Services—Online Marketing Plan" on pages 202 through 205.)

XYZ Advisory Services—Online Marketing Plan

(A) The top 20 percent of my customers

I HAVE A GENERAL PRACTICE with a mix of personal and business clients. I currently do not have a niche market. The top 20 percent of my existing customers have an average age of fifty-four; 42 percent are female; and they have an average income of $98,000 per year. However, about 3 percent have incomes in excess of $250,000. Over 60 percent of all my clients use the Internet on a regular basis, and 78 percent have an e-mail address. However, based on current trends, I expect use in both categories to continue to grow rapidly. About 20 percent of my target customers are of Latin heritage. This ethnic group is growing rapidly, at about 2 percent per year. My target group is active socially and to a lesser extent politically. Seventy-nine percent of this target group are located within the immediate metropolitan area, and 13 percent are located out of state.

1 External marketing environment. Unemployment generally runs about 7 percent. However, recently the ABC plant laid off 1,200 workers. These are generally blue-collar workers, with only about 10 percent in management. The EFD Corporation announced that it would be moving its electronics division to the outskirts of town at the beginning of next year. This should inject about 500 new employees into the local economy, at least half of whom will be highly compensated. It appears that at least 40 percent of the community will have access to high-bandwidth communications by the end of next year. In researching the Web, I could find only one direct local competitor with a Web site. However, a number of regional competitors with Web sites claim to service this metropolitan area (list is attached).

2 SWOT analysis. Existing clients generate more than 65 percent of my production. I have a loyal client base; my average customer has been with me for more than eight years. However, my client base is not growing very rapidly (2 percent per year, almost all of this due to referrals), and I have been able to increase sales to my existing base by only about 3 percent per year. Thus, although income is at a reasonably comfortable level, I am unable to generate much increase. I feel that my staff and I are not very efficient in handling customer service requests. Although my clients appear to be happy with my level of service, my assistant and I are spending too much time on routine operational questions, leaving little time for sales calls.

I have an excellent client management system; however, the current version of my system does not allow automated e-mails. I also do not employ any systematic means of collecting e-mail addresses for prospects or my existing clients. I have a business e-mail address, but I do not now regularly use e-mail as part of my marketing or service.

My current staff and I are very competent at handling the software and hardware needs of my office, but we do not have a sufficient understanding of how to use the Internet. I have a very primitive Web site that I had a local Internet service provider develop about a year ago. The results were disappointing—low traffic, no inquiries, and a somewhat unprofessional look to the site. I also tend to forget to update the site regularly, and the information posted is at times out-of-date. I have integrated my e-mail address and Web site address into my letterhead and marketing material, but I am inconsistent in referencing these channels.

The critical problems I need to overcome are to increase the efficiency of my office, to increase the number of new-client referrals, and to free up time to acquire new clients.

(B) The Plan
1 Online goal. By the end of next year I want at least 50 percent of my current client and prospect interactions online. I also want a 25 percent increase in new clients, at least 50 percent of that increase being from online contacts. I want at

(continued)

XYZ Advisory Services—Online Marketing Plan (continued)

least 20 percent of client inquiries to be handled via online content without my staff or me being involved.

2 Objectives

—Develop a new Web site (see "Web site development plan" for details.)

—Develop a mini site for online forms

—Upgrade contact management system with automated e-mail capability

—Collect e-mail addresses from current client base

—Configure contact management system to automatically send regular e-mails to all clients

—Send short personal e-mails for birthdays, holidays, anniversaries, graduations, or other events

—Send regular e-mails to the top 20 percent of my clients soliciting referrals

—Create and send a regular e-mail newsletter link (monthly or quarterly) to my clients

—Schedule a regular portfolio review e-mail reminder (semi-annual) with my clients

—Schedule an online portfolio review with all my clients, encouraging my remote and low-net-worth clients to use a Webcast

3 Online promotional and service plans.

My principal marketing vehicle will continue to be the annual portfolio review. I will increase both the number and quality of my client contacts by supplementing regular mailings with e-mail and e-mail newsletters. Client contacts will increase to once per month. I will strive to direct client inquiries to my new Web site. This will allow routine questions to be handled in an automated fashion online.

APPENDIX B

INTERNET
RESOURCES

Major Search Engines and Directories[1]

◆ **AltaVista** (http://www.altavista.com). AltaVista is consistently one of the largest search engines on the Web in terms of pages indexed. Its comprehensive coverage and wide range of power-searching commands make it a particular favorite among researchers. It also offers a number of features designed to appeal to basic users, such as "Ask AltaVista" results, which come from Ask Jeeves (see below), and directory listings from the Open Directory and LookSmart. AltaVista opened in December 1995. It was owned by Digital, then run by Compaq (which purchased Digital in 1998), then spun off into a separate company, which is now controlled by CMGI. AltaVista also operates the Raging Search service (see below).

◆ **AOL Search** (http://search.aol.com). AOL Search allows its members to search across the Web and AOL's own content from one place. The "external" version, listed above, does not list AOL content. The main listings for categories and Web sites come from the Open Directory (see below). Inktomi (see below) also provides crawler-based results as backup to the directory information. Before the launch of AOL Search in October 1999, the AOL search service was the Excite-powered AOL NetFind.

◆ **Ask Jeeves** (http://www.askjeeves.com). Ask Jeeves is a human-powered search service that aims to direct you to the exact page that answers your question. If it fails to find a match within its own database, then it will provide matching Web pages from various search engines. The service went into beta testing in mid-April 1997 and opened fully on June 1, 1997. Results from Ask Jeeves also appear within AltaVista.

◆ **Direct Hit** (http://www.directhit.com). Direct Hit is a company that works with other search engines to refine their results. It does this by monitoring what users click on from the results they see. Sites that get clicked on more than others rise higher in Direct Hit's rankings. Thus, the service dubs itself a "popularity engine." Direct Hit's technology is currently best seen at HotBot. It also refines results at Lycos and is available as an option at LookSmart and MSN Search. The company also crawls the Web and refines this database, which can be viewed via the link above.

◆ **Excite** (http://www.excite.com). Excite is one of the most popular search services on the Web. It offers a medium-sized index and integrates non-Web material such as company information and sports scores into its results, when appropriate. Excite was launched in late 1995. It grew quickly in prominence and consumed two of its competitors, Magellan in July 1996 and WebCrawler in November 1996. These continue to run as separate services.

◆ **FAST Search** (http://www.alltheweb.com). Formerly called All the Web, FAST Search aims to index the entire Web. It was the first search engine to break the 200 million Web page index milestone. The Norwegian company behind FAST Search also powers the Lycos MP3 search engine. FAST Search launched in May 1999.

◆ **Go** (http://www.go.com). Go is a portal site produced by Infoseek and Disney. It offers portal features such as personalization and free e-mail, plus the search capabilities of the former Infoseek search service, which has now been folded into Go. Searchers will find that Go consistently provides quality results in response to many general and broad searches, thanks to its ESP search algorithm. It also has an impressive human-compiled directory of Web sites. Go officially launched in January 1999. It is not related to GoTo (see below). The former Infoseek service launched in early 1995.

◆ **Google** (http://www.google.com). Google is a search engine that makes heavy use of link popularity as a primary way to rank Web sites. This can be especially helpful in finding good sites in response to general searches such as "cars" and "travel," because users across the Web have in essence voted for good sites by linking to them. The system works so well that Google has gained widespread praise for its high relevancy. Google also has a huge index of the Web and provides some results to Yahoo! and Netscape Search.

◆ **GoTo** (http://www.goto.com). Unlike the other major search engines, GoTo sells its main listings. Companies can pay money to be placed higher in the search results, which GoTo feels improves relevancy. Nonpaid results come from Inktomi (see below). GoTo launched in 1997 and incorporated the former University of Colorado–based World Wide Web Worm. In February 1998, it shifted to its current pay-for-placement model and soon after replaced the WWW Worm with Inktomi for its nonpaid listings. GoTo is not related to Go (Infoseek).

◆ **HotBot** (http://www.hotbot.com). HotBot is a favorite among researchers due to its many power-searching features. In most cases, HotBot's first page of results comes from the Direct Hit service (see above), and then secondary results come from the Inktomi search engine, which is also used by other services. It gets its directory information from the Open Directory project (see below). HotBot launched in May 1996 as Wired Digital's entry into the search engine market. Lycos purchased Wired Digital in October 1998 and continues to run HotBot as a separate search service.

◆ **Inktomi** (http://www.inktomi.com). Originally, there was an Inktomi search engine at the University of California, Berkeley. The creators then formed their own company with the same name and created a new Inktomi index, which was first used to power HotBot. Now the Inktomi index also powers several other services. All of them tap into the same index, though results may be slightly different. This is because Inktomi provides ways for its partners to use a common index yet distinguish themselves. There is no way to query the Inktomi index directly, as it is only made available through Inktomi's partners with whatever filters and ranking tweaks they may apply.

◆ **IWon** (http://www.iwon.com). Backed by U.S. television network CBS, iWon has a directory of Web sites generated automatically by Inktomi, which also provides its more traditional crawler-based results. iWon gives away daily, weekly, and monthly prizes in a marketing model unique among the major services. It launched in fall 1999.

◆ **LookSmart** (http://www.looksmart.com). LookSmart is a human-compiled directory of Web sites. In addition to being a stand-alone service, LookSmart provides directory results to MSN Search, Excite, and many other partners. AltaVista provides LookSmart with search results when a search fails to find a match from among LookSmart's reviews. Reader's Digest for about a year backed LookSmart, launched independently in October 1996, and then company executives bought back control of the service.

◆ **Lycos** (http://www.lycos.com). Lycos started out as a search engine, depending on listings that came from spidering the Web. In April 1999, it shifted to a directory model similar to Yahoo! Its main listings come from the Open Directory project, and then secondary results come from either Direct Hit or Lycos's own spidering of the Web. In October 1998, Lycos acquired the competing HotBot search service, which continues to be run separately.

◆ **MSN Search** (http://search.msn.com). Microsoft's MSN Search service is a LookSmart-powered directory of Web sites, with secondary results that come from AltaVista. RealNames and Direct Hit data are also made available. MSN Search also offers a unique way for Internet Explorer 5 users to save past searches.

◆ **NBCi** (http://www.NBCi.com). NBCi is a human-compiled directory of Web sites, supplemented by search results from Inktomi. Like LookSmart, it aims to challenge Yahoo! as the champion of categorizing the Web. Launched as Snap in late 1997, it is now backed by CNet and NBC.

◆ **Netscape Search** (http://search.netscape.com). Netscape Search's results come primarily from the Open Directory and Netscape's own Smart Browsing database, which does an excellent job of listing "official" Web sites. Secondary results come from Google. At the Netscape Netcenter portal site, other search engines are also featured.

◆ **Northern Light** (http://www.northernlight.com). Northern Light is another favorite search engine among researchers. It features one of the largest indexes of the Web, along with the ability to cluster documents by topic. Northern Light also has a set of "special collection" documents that are not readily accessible to search engine spiders. There are documents from thousands of sources, including newswires, magazines, and databases. Searching these documents is free, but there is a charge of up to $4 to view them. There is no charge to view documents on the public Web—only for those within the special collection. Northern Light opened to general use in August 1997.

◆ **Open Directory** (http://dmoz.org). The Open Directory uses volunteer editors to catalog the Web. Formerly known as NewHoo, it was launched in June 1998. Netscape acquired it in November 1998, and the company pledged that anyone would be able to use information from the directory through an open license arrangement. Netscape itself was the first licensee. Lycos and AOL Search also make heavy use of Open Directory data, while AltaVista and HotBot prominently feature Open Directory categories within their results pages.

◆ **Raging Search** (http://ragingsearch.altavista.com). Operated by AltaVista, Raging Search uses the same core index as AltaVista and virtually the same ranking algorithms. Why use it? AltaVista offers it for those who want fast search results, with no portal features getting in the way.

◆ **RealNames** (http://www.realnames.com). The RealNames system is meant to be an easier-to-use alternative to the current Web site addressing system. Those with RealNames-enabled browsers can enter a word like "Nike" to reach the Nike Web site. To date, RealNames has had its biggest success through search engine partnerships. See the Using RealNames Links page for more information about RealNames.

◆ **WebCrawler** (http://www.webcrawler.com). WebCrawler has the smallest index of any major search engine on the Web—think of it as Excite Lite. The small index means WebCrawler is not the place to go when seeking obscure or unusual material. However, some people feel that by having indexed fewer pages, WebCrawler provides less overwhelming results in response to general searches. WebCrawler opened to the public on April 20, 1994. It was started as a research project at the University of Washington. America Online purchased it in March 1995, and it was the online service's preferred search engine until November 1996, when Excite, a WebCrawler competitor, acquired the service. Excite continues to run WebCrawler as an independent search engine.

◆ **WebTop** (http://www.webtop.com). WebTop is a crawler-based search engine that claims an extremely large index. In addition to listing Web pages, WebTop also provides information from news sources, company information, and related content in its search results. The company also offers the WebCheck tool (formerly called k-check), which is a search and discovery tool. WebTop is backed by Bright Station, the company that acquired some search technology and other resources from the former Dialog Corporation. The Dialog search service itself is now owned by a different company, the Thomson Corporation.

◆ **Yahoo!** (http://www.yahoo.com). Yahoo! is the Web's most popular search service and has a well-deserved reputation for helping people find information easily. The secret to Yahoo!'s success is human beings. It is the largest human-compiled guide to the Web, employing about 150 editors in an effort to categorize the Web. Yahoo! lists more than 1 million sites. Yahoo! also supplements its results with those from Inktomi. If a search fails to find a match within Yahoo!'s own listings, then matches from Inktomi are displayed. Inktomi matches also appear after all Yahoo! matches have first been shown. Yahoo! is the oldest major Web-site directory, having launched in late 1994.

Research Sites

SINCE CURRENT ARTICLES can cover a wide range of financial subjects, I've included a number of diverse Internet sites covering economic, industry, market, company, and product research sources. Many of these sources can be used for developing your individual client recommendations. Some of these sites offer free research. Others contain summary information; if you want the full report, you must pay for it. Some of these sources are actually a listing of links to additional research sites.

Accenture (formerly Andersen Consulting) (http://www.accenture. com/index.html)

The Annual Reports Library (http://www.zpub.com/sf/arl)

Annuity.com (http://www.annuity.com)

Argus Research (http://www.argusresearch.com/main_content.html)

The Brookings Institution (http://www.brook.edu)

Business Intelligence Center (http://future.sri.com/index.shtml)

CMS (http://www.biz-lib.com/index.html)

Conning (http://www.conning.com)

Corporate Finance Network (http://www.corpfinet.com)

Dalbar, Inc. (http://www.dalbar.com)

Deloitte & Touche (http://www.dttus.com/PUB/default.htm)

The Dismal Scientist (http://www.dismal.com/forecasts/ forecasts.stm)

Dow Jones Interactive (http://djinteractive.com) and Ask Dow Jones (http://bis.dowjones.com)

Dun & Bradstreet (https://www.dnb.com/product/retail/ menu.htm)

Dun & Bradstreet's Companies Online (http://www.companieson line.com)

Edgar Online and FreeEDGAR (http://www.freeedgar.com)

Ernst & Young (http://www.ey.com/global/gcr.nsf/International/ Welcome_3)

Federal Reserve Financial Services section (http://www.frbser vices.org/Industry/MarketResearch.cfm)

Findex (http://www.findex.com)

Forrester Research (http://www.forrester.com)

The Heritage Foundation (http://www.heritage.org/library)

Hoovers (http://www.hoovers.com)

Horsesmouth (http://horsesmouth.com)

I/B/E/S International Inc. (http://www.ibes.com)

IPO.com initial public offerings site (http://www.ipo.com)

A. T. Kearney (http://www.atkearney.com)

KPMG (http://www.us.kpmg.com)

Mainspring Research (http://www.mainspring.com/home)

MarketGuide (http://www.marketguide.com/mgi/home.asp)

MarketResearch.com (http://www.marketresearch.com)

Moody's Investor Service (http://www.moodys.com)

Morningstar.com (http://www.morningstar.com/Cover/ Products.html)

Multex Investor Network independent investment research site (http://multex.com)

The National Information Center (http://www.ffiec.gov/ nic/default.htm)

NUA Internet Surveys (http://www.nua.ie/surveys)

Ohio State University (http://www.cob.ohio-state.edu/dept/ fin/overview.htm)

PricewaterhouseCoopers (http://www.pwcglobal.com/us/eng/ about/ind/index.html)

ProDevelop.Net (http://www.prodevelop.net)

Red Chip Review (http://www.redchip.com/Homepage.asp)

Reuters Moneynet (http://www.moneynet.com/home/ Moneynet/homepage/homepage.asp)

The Standard (http://www.thestandard.net)

Standard & Poor's Advisor Insight (http://www.advisorin sight.com)

Street Eye Investment Meta-Search Engine (http://www.street eye.com/cgi-bin/allseeingeye.cgi)

Thompson Financial (http://www.thomsonfinancial.com)

WallStreetTape.com (http://www.wallstreettape.com)

The Wharton School Financial Institutions Center (http://wrd senet.wharton.upenn.edu/fic/wfic.html)

XLS (http://www.xls.com)

WIRE HOUSE AND REGIONAL RESEARCH

Goldman Sachs (http://www.gsnews.com/index2.html)

Merrill Lynch (http://www.askmerrill.ml.com/mlol/main/ index.asp)

Morgan Stanley (http://www.msdw.com/index.html)

Robertson Stephens (http://www.robertstephens.com/research/ welcome.asp)

Salomon Smith Barney (http://www.smithbarney.com)

US Bancorp Piper Jaffray (http://www.gotoanalysts.com/piperpub lic/goto/index.asp)

PREFACE

1. "The Internet and Financial Product Distribution," Cerulli Associates, Inc., April 2000.

2. "One-Stop Shops Won't Cut It," Forrester, August 1, 1998. Three market segments profiled along with strategies to attract these customers (fifteen pages). Survey of representative sample of 120,000 North American households about how they buy and use technology. It follows up with in-depth interviews about the financial behavior of 6,000 who are online or have high income. Also conducted interviews with major financial services firms.

Found that prosperous GenXers, the emerging affluent, and the working affluent represent 60 percent of the current users of online financial services.

• Emerging affluent consumers (age 25–44, income $50–150K: 17 percent have investable assets > $250K, 74 percent own PCs) are the most important segment in the development of online financial services over the next five years. Emerging affluent have complicated financial lives, want to manage bank balances and securities online, and use the Net for utilitarian purposes. They represent 15 percent of households, 35 percent of wages, and 42 percent of those using online services.

• Prosperous GenXers (age 18–35, income $35–50K: 2 percent have investable assets > $250K, 55 percent own PCs) have simple financial lives but diverse online activity and a greater willingness to perform financial activities online. They represent 5 percent of households, 8 percent of wages, and 8 percent of those using online services.

• Like the emerging affluent, the working affluent (age 45–55, income > $75K: 45 percent have investable assets > $250K, 81 percent own PCs) have complicated financial lives, want to manage bank balances and securities online, and use the Net for utilitarian purposes. However, they are 50 percent more likely than the emerging affluent to have an existing relationship with a full-service brokerage. Almost 75 percent read a daily newspaper and are more willing to read business and finance magazines and watch cable news and business programs. They represent 5 percent of households, 10 percent of wages, and 10 percent of those using online services.

3. "Risk Tolerance and Life-Stage Marketing in Financial Services," Original Research Summary, SRI's CFD Marketing Report, April 1, 1999. Summary of changes in risk tolerance versus life stage and the impact on buying habits (two pages). Trend data between 1994 and 1998 show a significant overall increase in risk tolerance across all life stages, particularly among younger households with no children.

4. "The Affluent Move Their Money On-Line," Forrester research, February 1, 1999. eighteen pages. Analysis based on interviews and surveys of more than 2,600 North American households with investable assets, not including their homes, in excess of $750,000 (drawn from Forrester's Consumers & Technographics '99 Field Study of 94,200 North American households, completed in December 1998).

• Measured against any segment with less than $750,000 in investable assets, the affluent have the most positive attitudes about technology. More than one in three say that they like technology and that technology is important to them. The wealthier the consumer, the more positive he or she is likely to be.

• Forty-eight percent of affluent households in North America are online, versus 33 percent of the overall population. Eighty-six percent send e-mail, 79 percent surf the Web, and 46 percent research product purchases. Nearly half made purchases online—more than any other segment.

• Once online, the affluent are the most likely to view stock quotes, seek financial guidance, visit financial sites, and complete financial transactions. By year-end 1998, 10 percent of online affluent households traded with Internet-only brokerages—double that of the previous year.

Nineteen percent say they are likely to trade online in the next twelve months.

• Twenty-two percent of the affluent who trade online maintain more than half their portfolios with online firms. Of those who are online but have not yet traded, only half are held back by an allegiance to their existing broker.

CHAPTER 3: DIRECT E-MAIL MARKETING

1. Ray Jutkins, "The Online Advertising Report: Revenue Models, Strategies and Forecasts," *Jupiter Communications Research Study,* October, 1999.
2. Ray Jutkins, "Timeless Copy Appeals," ROCKINGHAM*JUTKINS *marketing.

CHAPTER 4: NICHE MARKETING

1. © 2000 Primelife, Orange, Calif.

CHAPTER 5: REACH OUT AND TOUCH SOMEONE

1. Thomas P. Novak and Donna L. Hoffman, "New Metrics for New Media: Toward the Development of Web Measurement Standards," Project 2000 (now called eLab), Vanderbilt University, September 26, 1996, www2000.ogsm.vanderbilt.edu.
2. Ibid.
3. "An Advertising Primer: Terminology, Traffic, Statistics and Usage," *Ad Resource,* September 14, 1999.
4. Ibid.
5. Steve Lawrence and Lee Giles, "Accessibility and Distribution of Information on the Web," *Nature,* 400: 107-109, 1999.
6. Kip Gregory, "Take Aim at the Internet: 12 Steps for Working the Web to Build Better Relationships," © 2000 The Gregory Group, http://www.gregory-group.com.

CHAPTER 6: WHAT MAKES A GOOD SITE GOOD?

1. These tips are a compilation from my own experience and a number of online sources, including: Ken Fermoyle, "Design Do's & Don'ts: How to Look Good in Print," © 1998 by Ken Fermoyle, Fermoyle Publications; Web Graphics Notes, "Design Do's and Don'ts," by Paladin Computer Services; "Design Tips, Do's & Don'ts," © 1998 Intraconnect Inc.; Internet Design,

"Food for Thought When Designing Your Web-Site," ©1996 Internet Schoolhouse.

2. "Trends in RAI and Internet Distribution," workshop presented to Securities America April 3, 2000, Cerulli Associates, Inc.

3. The smallest element of an image that can be individually processed in a video display system.

CHAPTER 7: WEB SITE DEVELOPERS

1. These tips are a compilation from my own experience and Sandra Duban, "Hiring a Web-Site Developer," Command Line Computer Services, www.duban.com.

CHAPTER 8: MARKETING AND PROMOTING YOUR WEB SITE

1. Principal source is "Meta Tag Information," © 1996–2000 Viper, Inc.

2. Principal source is "Submit Corner: ALT Image Tags," © 1999 Wired 2000 Corporation Inc., http://www.submitcorner.com/Guide/Improve/altimage.shtml.

CONCLUSION

1. Jennifer Franklin, Dan Latimore, and David Morris, "Retail Brokers Say the Internet Is Just Another Tool of the Trade," *eStrategy Report,* Mainspring, July 31, 2000.

APPENDIX B

1. Danny Sullivan, "The Major Search Engines," Search Engine Watch, http://searchenginewatch.com, © 1996–2000 internet.com Corp.

About Bloomberg

Bloomberg L.P., founded in 1981, is a global information services, news, and media company. Headquartered in New York, the company has 9 sales offices, 2 data centers, and 79 news bureaus worldwide.

Bloomberg, serving customers in 100 countries around the world, holds a unique position within the financial services industry by providing an unparalleled range of features in a single package known as the BLOOMBERG PROFESSIONAL™ service. By addressing the demand for investment performance and efficiency through an exceptional combination of information, analytic, electronic trading, and Straight Through Processing tools, Bloomberg has built a worldwide customer base of corporations, issuers, financial intermediaries, and institutional investors.

BLOOMBERG NEWS℠, founded in 1990, provides stories and columns on business, general news, politics, and sports to leading newspapers and magazines throughout the world. BLOOMBERG TELEVISION®, a 24-hour business and financial news network, is produced and distributed globally in seven different languages. BLOOMBERG RADIO™ is an international radio network anchored by flagship station BLOOMBERG® WBBR 1130 in New York.

In addition to the BLOOMBERG PRESS® line of books, Bloomberg publishes *BLOOMBERG® MARKETS, BLOOMBERG PERSONAL FINANCE™,* and *BLOOMBERG® WEALTH MANAGER.* To learn more about Bloomberg, call a sales representative at:

Frankfurt:	49-69-92041-200	São Paulo:	5511-3048-4530
Hong Kong:	85-2-2977-6600	Singapore:	65-212-1200
London:	44-20-7330-7500	Sydney:	61-2-9777-8601
New York:	1-212-318-2200	Tokyo:	81-3-3201-8950
San Francisco:	1-415-912-2980		

FOR IN-DEPTH MARKET INFORMATION and news, visit BLOOMBERG.COM®, which draws from the news and power of the BLOOMBERG PROFESSIONAL™ service and Bloomberg's host of media products to provide high-quality news and information in multiple languages on stocks, bonds, currencies, and commodities, at **www.bloomberg.com.**

About the Author

Douglas H. Durrie is the former vice president of industry research and intelligence for Securities America Financial Corporation. With more than twenty years' experience in marketing and research, Doug has worked on numerous marketing initiatives, particularly those involving technology. He has coordinated public relations, corporate advertising, and marketing planning. He has also developed Web site strategies and coordinated Internet marketing and communications for Securities America's family of companies.

About Securities America Financial Corporation

Securities America Financial Corporation, a wholly owned subsidiary of American Express Financial Corporation and a sister company of American Express Financial Advisors, Inc., is the parent company of Securities America, Inc., a national broker-dealer, and Securities America Advisors, Inc., a provider of fee-based asset management services to Registered Investment Advisors nationwide. Together, these organizations support and service the entrepreneurial activities of independent financial representatives. With more than 1,300 financial representatives throughout the United States, Securities America focuses on providing an array of dynamic online technology, innovative practice management, professional-development support, extensive products and services from premier financial companies, and flexible fee-based programs to meet the diverse needs of today's marketplace.